RABBINIC AUTHORITY

PAPERS PRESENTED BEFORE THE
NINETY-FIRST ANNUAL CONVENTION
OF THE CENTRAL CONFERENCE OF
AMERICAN RABBIS

RABBINIC AUTHORITY

PAPERS PRESENTED BEFORE THE
NINETY-FIRST ANNUAL CONVENTION
OF THE CENTRAL CONFERENCE OF
AMERICAN RABBIS

VOLUME XC
PART TWO

EDITED BY ELLIOT L. STEVENS

CENTRAL CONFERENCE OF AMERICAN RABBIS
21 EAST 40TH STREET
NEW YORK, NY 10016

Library of Congress Cataloging in Publication Data
Main entry under title:

Rabbinic authority.

(Yearbook, ISSN 0069-1607 ; v. 90, pt. 2)
Bibliography: p.
1. Rabbis—Office—Addresses, essays, lectures.
2. Reform Judaism—Addresses, essays, lectures.
3. Jewish law—Reform Judaism—Addresses, essays,
lectures. I. Stevens, Elliot. II. Central
Conference of American Rabbis. III. Series: Yearbook (Central Conference of American Rabbis) ;
v. 90, pt. 2.
BM30.C4 vol. 90, pt. 2   [BM652]   296'.0973s   82-12628
ISBN 0-916694-88-7   [296.6'1]

PRINTED IN THE UNITED STATES OF AMERICA

Central Conference of American Rabbis

21 East 40th Street

New York, N.Y. 10016

TABLE OF CONTENTS

PREFACE

Is rabbinic authority based solely on the contemporary rabbi's powers of persuasion in generating communal support? What role, if any, do a rabbi's scholarly attainments or moral stance play as determinants of that rabbi's sense of authenticity? How is the authority of a rabbi affected by his or her personal religion? How should the sense of rabbinic authority be made manifest in a particular Jewish community, or vis-à-vis gentiles with whom the rabbi might have professional contact?

The Program Committee of the Central Conference of American Rabbis, in preparing for the 1980 CCAR convention in Pittsburgh, elected to offer a broad variety of Torah courses relating directly or tangentially to the overall convention theme: Rabbinic Authority. Twenty rabbis, among them scholars teaching at Hebrew Union College–Jewish Institute of Religion and at other academic institutions, as well as thoughtful colleagues from the congregational rabbinate, each prepared a two-hour course on some question of rabbinic authority. Thirteen of these convention faculty then responded to an invitation to submit articles for the present volume. The volume—in effect Part II of the 1980 *CCAR Yearbook*—includes as well the two major papers, which addressed the theme's broader perspectives, and which in turn served as the basis for much of the ensuing convention discussion.

The papers published herein were submitted in a variety of styles. Some represent transcripts of "live" offerings at the convention itself. Two are outlines which were distributed to course participants, where submission of a full paper proved impractical. One is a reprinted paper originally published in a European scholarly journal; the rest were newly written for this volume.

Despite minimal editorial efforts toward stylistic consistency, the broad divergency of the submissions militated against the imposing of artificial stylistic norms. The authors' papers and outlines have, rather, been allowed to speak for themselves, together covering a substantial proportion of those issues usually subsumed under the general heading of rabbinic authority. For those wishing to engage in further study, a selected bibliography has been added.

The editor wishes to thank Mr. Irving Ruderman of KTAV Publishing House, Inc., for his personal concern and helpful involvement in the editorial process, and for his meticulous attention to detail.

Elliot L. Stevens
March 1982

RABBINIC AUTHORITY: AN OVERVIEW

VINEYARDS OF THE LORD

Jerome R. Malino

רעי, יקירי, שותפי בעבודת הקדוש —

Beloved friends, partners in sacred endeavor—a decade has passed since our attention was forcefully brought to a consideration of the unsettling consequences of change, and most especially, of the consequences of the accelerating rate of change which presents an additional psychological obstacle to coming to terms with the real world about us. Toffler speaks of the "roaring current of change, a current so powerful today, that it overturns institutions, shifts our values and shrivels our roots." The discerning individual surely does not need Toffler's marshaling of data to be persuaded to the truth of his observation. The evidence is everywhere about us and the effects are to be read in the lives of people in every walk of society and in every community. Even if the Jewish people are not, as has once been observed, "like everyone else only more so," they must respond, as do all others, to the world about them with the added responsibility of maintaining their own communal identity and preserving their own unique value system.

In all of the foregoing, the role of the rabbis is critical. No one is more intimately involved in the lives of people than the rabbi who shares, and often directs, the circumstances of their personal lives and the character of the institution which expresses their collective aspiration and is a manifestation of their collective identity. The rabbi is an essential part of a people which has itself always been a barometer of social, intellectual, political, and economic change. As a part of this people he is subject, as all of them are, to the same forces that have such an unsettling impact on our lives. Together with others, the rabbi must deal with change, but has the added responsibility of helping to share the consequences of the change in his effort to maintain the vibrant and meaningful continuity of Jewish life. The rabbi's calling, the rabbi's vocation, if you will, his training and learning, draw their inspiration from the teachings and the experiences of the past and from the age-old Jewish preoccupation with the abiding and the enduring. Not only is the rabbi subjected to the buffeting of the times, he is also challenged by an agonizing search for the contemporary relevance of what is the sum and substance of the rabbi's being. Not content merely with finding his own way, he will insist on guiding others through the shadowy darkness.

On the larger American scene we have witnessed a radical change in the structure of religious life. A rampant secularism is paradoxically accompanied by a radical fundamentalism. The former undermines decades of interreligious dialogue and cooperation, while the latter mars the very language and vocabulary of interreligious communication. An intensified parochialism and a preoccupation with institutional well-being have replaced the optimism of the past and its hope for a spiritualizing impact on American life and culture.

The conventional values that were an integral part of the "American way of

life" for more than two centuries have been subjected to revolutionary change
at worst, or to a relativistic indifference at best. We are a country on the move,
denied the stability and the rootedness that comes from long association with
place and people. There is a wavering uncertainty in America about our role on
the world scene, about the direction and the purpose of American democracy
and about the trustworthiness of the principles which, in the past, we assumed
to be the foundations of American greatness.

The Jewish world has always reflected, with heightened intensity, the
patterns of life in the larger world in which the Jew lived. If the Jew *is* "like
everyone else only more so," it is nowhere more apparent than in the way
contemporary Jewish life has been affected by the vagaries and the shifting
values of the American scene. There is a growing secularism in Jewish life that
is not belied by the numbers of the synagogue affiliated. Many Jews are not
affiliated with a religious institution, and even those who are so affiliated, for the
most part, live lives that are completely secular in character; nor are they
responsive to the spiritual and religious mandates of Judaism. We have seen the
direction of Jewish life resting in the hands of secular Jewish institutions with
the only institutional representation of Jewish religious life in this country
being treated disdainfully when it is not ignored.

There was a time when Jews lived together for security's sake and in order to
be better able to fulfill the requirements of a demanding religious discipline. The
mobility in the lives of contemporary Jews has profound psychological and
institutional implications. The Jewish family, once far-reaching and immeasurably supportive, has been reduced, like the family in general, to its nuclear
dimensions. This is bad enough for the country as a whole; it is immeasurably
worse for a community that relied on generational continuity for the preserva-
tion of its most vital life-patterns. For a while, the shift of Jewish population
from the urban to the suburban scene made it possible for Jews to find within the
synagogue community some modest replacement for the intensity of intimate
family association. But here, too, we are witnessing radical change with the
suburban synagogue losing much of its influence with the mobile young and with
a growing shift of the older Jewish population back to the cities. I will leave to
others the dismal calculation of the effect of zero population growth which we
have achieved, much sooner than others, and with consequences of a far more
serious nature.

The rabbi of today confronts all of the foregoing with a sensitive awareness of
the dichotomy between the rabbi's training and the rabbi's role. More than two
and a half decades ago, before many of the noted changes had yet taken place,
our colleague Bernard Bamberger, so recently deceased and so deeply
mourned, עליו השלום, observed, "The American rabbi is a novel and unique
phenomenon in Jewish experience. His office is related to the earliest forms of
Jewish life by a tie of historic continuity; yet the modern rabbinate presents so
radical a change both in function and in temper as to constitute a virtually new
profession."

Surely it is not surprising if, under these circumstances, there should be a
genuine malaise in the American rabbinate. It is even greater in the Liberal or
Reform wing of the American rabbinate where the tradition is more liberating

than confining and where the responsibility is ever present for seeking out and developing new approaches to the problems of contemporary life. It is imperative, under such circumstances, that we give most careful consideration to who we are and what we are; that we pursue the path to self-understanding in order that we might effectively deal with the needs of our people, apply the criteria of our religious tradition and fulfill our own role as vehicles of the Torah and its prophetic mandate. If we put aside, for the moment, the consideration of the vast social and moral issues that confront the world today, it is not out of disdain for those issues, nor out of a lack of awareness of our own critical responsibility to pass judgment on our times, but only because we understand that our judgments can be valid only to the extent that we are blessed with self-knowledge and self-understanding. We withdraw for the moment only that we might more resolutely confront our sacred responsibilities, our personal motivations and the demands of our office fortified by a fresh insight.

II

Doubt is not only understandable, it is therapeutic. The number is legion of those of our predecessors, prophetic and rabbinic, who agonized over the uncertainty of their own worth or the monumental character of the responsibilities that rested on their shoulders. Moses, Isaiah, Jeremiah, were at times overcome by a sense of their own unworthiness and were able, only through the deepest probing of their own psyches and through drawing on their own vast reservoir of faith, to rise to the heights of the human spirit that made their ministries possible.

And with whom shall we pursue their task but with one another גנאי הוא (תדבא״ר י״ז) לרב שיבכה לפני תלמידיו "shameful is it for the rabbi that he weep before his disciples." We cannot bare our deep problems or our own uncertainties before the people to whom we minister. We need the supportive presence of those who grapple as do we with the same gnawing doubts that exercise our own spirits.

Perhaps Rabbi Gamliel will forgive me if I attempt a paraphrase of his injunction (אבות א׳ ט״ז) עשה לך רב והסתלק מן הספק which might be made to read, "Get a rabbi for yourself that you might act forthrightly and without hesitation." As Moses confronted the people in a difficult and trying situation at the waters of Meribah, we are told by the Midrash, he stood in doubt and said, "If I hearken to them, then I deny the words of God." What was the denial of God? Was it yielding to the will of the people or persisting in uncertainty and doubt? Therapeutic and understandable as doubt may be, it cries out for resolution so that we and the Children of Israel might go forward.

What will emerge from our exercise will be a clearer self image. Far more important than how we appear to other is how we appear to ourselves. We minister constantly to the needs of other lives and must look to the needs of our own spirits. In commenting on the verse in Proverbs (12:10), יודע צדיק נפש בהמתו "A righteous man has regard for the life of his beast," the medieval commentator Caspi observed, "Who tends to himself as to his cattle will never be sick." We must look after ourselves no less than we look after the well-being of our flock. Ben Sira provides us with the penetrating observation that, "A man may be shrewd and a teacher of many, and yet be unprofitable to himself." Classical antiquity could find no loftier admonition to inscribe at Delphi than the well-known imperative, "Know thyself."

Reinforced by self knowledge we will be able to move to our task. Our study of ourselves is not, and will not be, a narcissistic indulgence but an inventory of our profound potential. Not for our own sake but for the sake of our families, for our people's sake, for the sake of our sacred calling we will study ourselves.

> More skillful in self knowledge, even more pure
> As tempted more; more able to endure
> As more exposed to suffering and distress
> Then also, more alive to tenderness.
> —*Wordsworth: "Character of the Happy Warrior"*

III

There is a letter written during the eighteenth century by one of the rabbis who served the Sephardic Jewish community of Bordeaux to the representative *intendant* of the king which has a painful poignancy and a sadly contemporary quality.

> If his Grace, the *Intendant,* would be so kind as to take the trouble to make a small reprimand to the heads of the Portuguese nation about the lack of respect and deference that they have for their Rabbi, all and sundry would be all the more thankful for his kindness in view of the resulting law and order.
> Since the life of his greatness is far above that of the suppliant, he will know what means to take and what pretext to use without making the reprimand appear to have been solicited.

See the dismal picture: a rabbi appealing to a non-Jewish authority to intercede with his own *baale-batim* because of the lack of respect and deference which they have for him and sadly suggesting that he might know better than the writer how best to acquire for the rabbi the respect and deference he sought.

It is indeed an ancient story. Over the centuries, those who have presumed to speak in God's name were sometimes hated, sometimes reviled, and often disregarded. Did not Ezekiel instruct himself, in God's name, to be prepared for precisely that disregard of the man and his message?

> As for you, son of man, your people who talk together about you by the walls and the doors of their houses, say to one another, each to his brother, "Come, and hear what the word is that comes forth from the Lord." And they come to you as people come, and they sit before you as my people, and they hear what you say, but they will not do it; for with their lips they show much love, but their heart is set on their gain. And, lo, you are to them like one who sings love songs with a beautiful voice and plays well on an instrument, they hear what you say but they will not do it.

And the Talmud goes so far as to say כל מקום שיש בו חלול השם אין חולקין כבוד לרב (עירובין סג:) "In whatever place there is a profanation of God's name, they do not show deference to the rabbi."

In another context of our Conference the authority of the rabbi will be examined in breadth and in depth. I am certain that this will be of immeasurable worth to all our colleagues and will be of continuing benefit for years to come. I will, nevertheless, allow myself a few observations borne of my own personal experience of four and a half decades in the rabbinate.

Authority is not procured by insisting on it but through the exercise of it. Nor need we exercise power in order to exert influence; the influence that derives from being the exponent of Jewish values and Jewish learning. So long as we truly represent the tradition in whose name we speak by the breadth of our knowledge and the integrity of our persons, we will exert a pervasive influence which no one will be able to diminish. We read, "When a father waives the deference due him it is waived. When a rabbi chooses to waive the deference due him the deference is not waived." This is a way of telling us that nothing can compromise the dignity of the rabbi, but Rabbi Joseph cautions us promptly and says, (קדושין לב.) אפילו הרב שמחל על כבודו, כבודו מחול "even a rabbi will find the deference due him waived if he chooses to waive that deference." I am, of course, not suggesting pomposity or exaggerated distance between rabbi and congregant, but I have never forgotten the caveat of Samson Benderly, who told us rabbinical students a half century ago, "If you want to raise another person, do not get lower than your knees." Our authority does not derive from our ordination or our diploma but from the tradition in whose name we speak. Let us *be* challenged. It matters not, so long as we are sustained by the strength and power of our tradition. If we take a strong position on a social issue and our people want to reject what we say, they should have to reject Amos and the full weight of the prophetic tradition as well.

IV

אם אין קמח אין תורה "Where there is no meal there is no Torah." The rabbi and his family are not immune to the currents of the economic world. The rabbi must feed and clothe the rabbi's family, must see to an appropriate educational experience for the rabbi's children. The rabbi must live in respectable dignity and must be able to provide for the satisfaction of those intellectual and aesthetic desires which have been cultivated through a long and intense educational experience. The compensation, therefore, which the rabbi receives, is a necessary ingredient for personal fulfillment and the fulfillment of the ambitions of the rabbi's family. The rabbi has perfectly proper and legitimate concerns regarding tenure and security. The rabbi must be protected against arbitrary and willful dismissal by the whole weight of our Conference influence. The operation of our placement procedures and the details of our pension plan must be continually examined and modified to assure a maximum benefit in stability and security for the members of our Conference. Having said this, and even at the risk of evoking criticism, I must insist that there is no substitute in the performance of rabbinic duties for conscientiousness, integrity, fullness of preparation, relentless pursuit of learning, and respect for the members of our congregations and the circumstances of their lives. Allow me to quote a sentence or two from a Conference sermon presented by our colleague Roland Gittelsohn in 1958. In speaking of the "struggle for economic survival" he said, "We rabbis are in an exceptionally favorable position in this regard. True, we don't grow rich in our profession nor are we by any means immune from the fluctuations of the economic barometer. But neither are we as immediately and directly affected by a multitude of daily business factors as are many of our members. Our economic seismographs are nowhere near as sensitive to the slightest industrial or financial tremor as are theirs." What does disturb me is the risk we run and to which we sometimes succumb, in judging our professional success by the criteria of the marketplace. We dare not allow ourselves to measure our success by the same criteria that determine the success of an economic or business enterprise. Alas for any rabbi who enters the profession with the purpose of achieving affluence. He is doomed either to disappointment or to a corruption of his rabbinic purpose. And even as we must be sure not to measure our professional success by the criteria of the marketplace, so must we also abstain from measuring our professional success by a needless comparison between the emoluments we receive and those from which some of our colleagues may benefit. I am not insensitive to the desire on the part of many for salary surveys and an analysis of fringe benefits, but if these things are going to create discontent where there should be a rich sense of personal and professional fulfillment, then surveys are an error. I am completely in favor of achieving a maximum available material reward for all of our colleagues. I worry only about the corruption of purpose when there is a preoccupation with the *kemach*.

The problem of compensation becomes a special concern in the light of lack of upward mobility for most of our colleagues and in the light of the fact that most of our colleagues will finish their careers in congregations of under 300 families. Sixty-three percent of the rabbis now serving congregations are in congregations of fewer than 300 families or are in assistantships. Add to this the distressing information that in the last five years only two rabbis over the age of fifty were able to move to larger congregations. How shall we look upon this fact of contemporary rabbinic life? Perhaps I may be allowed, by virtue of my own rabbinic experience, to comment personally on the present situation. I have stayed for forty-five years, not without alternative choices, in a small city and with a congregation which only now has achieved a membership of 450 families, but which, for most of my rabbinic career, had fewer than 300 families and for the first twenty years fewer than 200. The testimony I bear is not born of frustration, nor is it the result of the specious rationalization of an inability to do other than I have done. It derives altogether, and without reservation, from my full appreciation of the spiritual, professional, and human advantages of serving in a small community over a long and extensive ministry.

In his well-known book *Small Is Beautiful*, E. F. Schumacher has shown how our pursuit of bigness has compromised and threatened the most cherished values of the good society. In the aesthetic world, as in the world of moral values, bigness is irrelevant when it is not dangerous. I am inclined to agree with the denotation that small can most certainly be beautiful, and where it applies to the rabbinic career can be every bit as rewarding as a large metropolitan ministry, possessing qualities that can be duplicated nowhere else. Two testimonies to this conclusion come to my mind. One of them is a lecture which our late and esteemed colleague Abraham J. Feldman gave to the students of the Hebrew Union College just over forty years ago. Out of my own experience, I recall a paper which I presented before this Conference in 1947 on "The Pastoral Ministry in a Small City." So apt for our own time are the conclusions reached in the aforesaid presentations that the temptation is strong to quote extensively from them. I refer you to them and will here content myself with a brief listing of the enriching and challenging elements in the rabbinic ministry in a small city.

In a small city the Jewish community is preeminently a religious community and not a group of individuals identified by ethnic distinctiveness. Whether out of personal inclination or due to the general pattern of small city life, Jews find themselves drawn to the synagogue as an expression of their Jewish identification. This enhancement of the synagogue and its role is reflected in the regard held for the rabbi by the non-Jewish community which looks upon him as the Jewish authority par excellence, and turns to him as "their rabbi," a designation I have gratefully received over the years from Christian laity and clergy. The press is more responsive, as are the radio and television if there be one, and the opportunity is readily present for the rabbi to reach an audience that goes far beyond the borders of his own synagogue and congregation. As a citizen of the community, the rabbi is able to bring his talents to play on a whole host of community activities. Here, too, I pray that I may be indulged a personal reference when I speak of my twenty years on the local Board of Education and my involvement in such diverse enterprises as the Concert Association, the Music Centre, the Human Relations Commission, the Charter Revision Commission of the city of my residence and a chaplaincy for four decades in a federal penal institution.

A small city is a wonderful place to rear a family and a splendid environment in which to convey to children the unique and abiding elements of our rich Jewish tradition.

The rabbi in a small city will have time for study on his own, and, if there is an institution of higher learning in the area, in the pursuit of an advanced degree.

Perhaps the most rewarding aspect is the opportunity for abiding personal relationships, surely not unique to the small city, but most assuredly present in greater intensity even if in lesser quantity than in the large city and congregation. I am able, without hesitation and after forty-five years, to utter the same prayer of gratitude I spoke after twelve years in my pulpit when I said the rabbi "will feel himself a partner with God in creating souls. As he confirms those he knew as infants, marries those he has confirmed, as he sees his handiwork in happier and better integrated lives, as he grows with his labors and earns the love of those he served he will say, לפום צערא אגרא, 'the reward has been worthy the effort.' He will know that each year's experience equips him the better to face the next one and he will pray with Jacob, קטנתי מכל החסדים 'I am unworthy all the kindnesses that have been shown me.' "

I would wish, if I could, to reverse the tendency of many to see professional advancement only in terms of size either of membership or renumeration. One does not determine the merit of a work of art by taking its dimensions. Some miniaturists and illuminators of manuscripts have poured more intensity of color and feeling into their modestly proportioned exercises than have graced large murals. And if we conclude, nevertheless, that the circumstances of our professional lives deny us adventure and mobility, let us be able to say with Joseph: (Gen. 50:20) ואתם חשבתם עלי רעה, אלהים חשבה לטובה "Though you may have intended it for evil, God intended it for good."

V

I have, I hope understandably, put great emphasis on the rabbi in a small community. Let me now make at least passing reference to some of the personal and professional concerns of all rabbis.

We are cautioned against assigning too great importance to ourselves. We are reminded that nine rabbis do not constitute a *minyan* but ten shoemakers do. It is an appropriate distinction, but it does not obscure the fact that although the rabbi is just another Jew in some ways, his labors and his position produce concerns that are distinct to the rabbi. These concerns will be the substance of our seminars and our practica and I am confident that the participants will be both enlightened and enriched.

For the most part, the rabbi is alone. Should he have the companionship of other rabbis at regional meetings, *Kallot,* or within his own community, he is alone as he relates to the responsibilities of his office; alone indeed, precisely when he is most busily engaged with large numbers of people socially, religiously or in the teaching of Torah. This inescapable distinctiveness which is the rabbi's is shared as well by his family, which must endure not only the demands made on the person of the rabbi, his time and energy, but also their own unique status and distinctiveness in the life of the congregation and the community. "These are the rabbi's children," "this is the rabbi's husband or wife." Such are the designations that take the place of the conventional names by which others are known. Special skills are needed by the rabbi and in an age in which professionalization has become more and more specialized in medicine, the law and the sciences, there is imposed on the rabbi the need for a widening variety of skills and a competence is expected in an ever-increasing number of intellectual and professional disciplines. There is a risk for the rabbi in all this, for he may be distracted and diverted from "that one talent it is death to hide." The rabbi's domain is the Torah and nothing may take its place in the rabbi's life. There are no skills and no intellectual exercises that can justify a failure on the part of the rabbi to "set a fixed time for the study of Torah." This is our life and the length of our days and there can be no justification, if we are to continue to warrant the name rabbi, for a failure to probe ever more deeply into the limitless treasures of our intellectual tradition. No one will master the whole of Torah, but though we will not complete the task we are never free to desist from the pursuit of it.

The continuing study of Torah and the rabbi's personal faith are, alike, preeminent among the rabbi's concerns. Heaven itself knows that we are blessed, or afflicted, with a limitless array of theological concepts. The Central Conference of American Rabbis, able to agree on so many things, even the text of our new prayerbook, could not find a basis for common theological understanding. But within this boundless variety there must be a constant for the rabbi. God is! And within the limits of our finite talents and intellects we can sense the presence of the Divine. To bring that sense into the lives of others requires the continued cultivation, on the rabbi's part, of such awareness in his own life and experience. The prophets preached in the gates but found strength in solitude, in their intimate confrontation with the transcendent within themselves. It is so easy for the rabbi, who ministers to the religious needs of others, to overlook the nourishment of his own soul. I am not sure what conclusion to draw from the absence of our colleagues from our services of worship, from the need of a calculated ruse at our conventions, to combine Torah session with prayer, from the absence of *motzi* and *birkat hamazon* at our meals together, but I sense a lack of spirituality. It may be a reflection of the times, it may even be due to a measure of self-consciousness in our iconoclastic and skeptical world, but we cannot afford it. We may have our feet firmly planted on the earth, but we must, like Jacob's ladder, let our heads reach heavenward. Only then can angelic traffic join heaven and earth in holy communion. Changes of time and place may modify the activities of the rabbi, preaching and pastoral counseling may wax or wain, some things will have altered emphasis, some may disappear and new ones emerge, but the rabbi must remain unchanged as the repository of and the spokesman for and the renewer of the essence of Jewish faith and the values it implies. אלי, אלי, שלא יגמר לעולם "My God, my God, let this never cease to be."

Even as I underscore, and I think rightly, the importance of Torah and faith, I am yet mindful of the rabbinic caution, כל העוסק בתורה בלבד דומה כמי שאין לו אלוה (עבודה זרה יז:) "Whoever engages exclusively in the study of Torah is like one who has no God!"

The Central Conference of American Rabbis, with its long and distinguished concern with social issues, will surely continue to be sensitive to the Jewish responsibility of refashioning the world in a manner consistent with God's kingdom. We must never be distracted by a narrow parochialism or a passionate nationalism from the need to labor on behalf of the human condition. We who have so ably begun the mitzvah of social concern can only be encouraged to pursue it further.

Israel will remain preeminent among our interests not only where its security, sovereignty, and material well-being are at stake, but above all, where the quality and character of Israeli life are involved. The dream of Israel as a cultural center has known only partial realization. Jewry throughout the world has been a blessed beneficiary of the revitalization of Hebrew culture, the development of the Hebrew language and the enlargement of traditional and modern Jewish studies. But we have also seen a politicized religion growing in power and in influence and a failure on the part of the government of Israel to assure complete religious freedom to all Jews. The struggle on behalf of Liberal and Progressive Judaism in Israel, and the rights of Jews who profess other forms of their faith than are considered ritually acceptable to the two chief rabbinates, must be relentlessly pursued. The State of Israel is the achievement of world Jewry, and our stake in the direction it will take, though different from those who live in the Land, is not less intense, nor is it to be less passionately defended. The World Union for Progressive Judaism, our instrument for touching the hearts and minds of Jews everywhere in the world, warrants a greater support both material and spiritual, than we have been giving it. I would urge upon us all to sustain our movement in this country and wherever there are Jews. It is the most helpful device for stemming the tide of secularism among those who otherwise are without alternative to the Orthodox manifestation of the Jewish faith.

Our voices must be raised as well against violation in Israel, by government, party, or people, of the exalted ethical teachings of Judaism. Of what use is a state of our own if it bear testimony, not to righteousness and the pursuit of peace, but to expediency and maneuvering for political advantage. The Talmud tells us Jerusalem was destroyed because of a personal and petty feud between Kamtza and Bar Kamtza. Personal rivalries and political feuding are much too common phenomena in Israel. Whether in its domestic operation or its relationship to the Arab population, within and outside Israel, to profess to be ככל הגויים or to be content to be "like any other nation" is a betrayal of the Zionist dream and a denial of God.

Much has been said about the growing number of women rabbis in our movement, and steps have been taken to improve the prospects of placement for our women colleagues in pulpits and other areas of rabbinic endeavor. Our task forces on women in the rabbinate and in Jewish leadership generally are actively engaged in the practical steps we hope ultimately will lead to the full and unqualified integration of women rabbis in American Jewish life. But there is much that the male members of our Conference can do that is not being done. We must, each of us, take upon himself the responsibility of altering the climate within his own congregation if that climate is not congenial to the goals we have set ourselves. Not only when a female rabbi is candidating for a rabbinic post must the issue be drawn, but from day to day, even without such candidacies, we must press the importance of Torah and not sex in establishing the rabbi's worth or status. I would call upon every male member of our Conference to labor without rest until all distinctions based on sex have been removed. Every one of us is diminished when our female colleagues fail to receive the respect and the opportunity which we would aspire to for ourselves.

VI

The revelation of Sinai is not ended. The voice heard then is speaking still. Our Talmud tells us that prophecy was taken from the prophets and given to the rabbis. In response to the query, "Are not the rabbis prophets, too?" the answer given is that prophecy has not been taken from them. Once God's Presence left the Holy Mountain, Sinai reverted to just another high place. This prompted the rabbis to observe that "a person's place does not honor him but the person honors the place he is in " (*Taanit* 21b). The rabbinate does not honor us but allows us to bring honor to the rabbinate. We are called the מלאכי השרת (נדרים :כ)"the angels who minister to the Divine presence." We are the vehicles through which the *Shechinah* can be made visible to the people in our care.

Go forth, dear colleagues, to study and to teach. We read (*Pes.* 112a) "more than the calf wishes to suck, the cow needs to suckle." We are engaged in a timeless enterprise, as our colleague Jacob Neusner has observed. "However much the contemporary Rabbi differs from the Rabbi of antiquity and medieval times, far more does he continue in roles and tasks they began. He measures himself by knowledge of Torah, and so do the people, although they may claim otherwise. He stands apart from others yet above them in ways that are not at all secular. In the midst of this world and its concerns, he represents another realm of being. People know it; they expect it; they demand it." In this timeless enterprise we can take it to heart the words of Yehuda Ha-Levi:

> Servants of time are slaves of slaves
> The Servant of God alone is free.
> When each one therefore seeks his lot
> My soul saith, "God my lot shall be."

(Nu. 10:35) ויהי בנסוע הארון "And when the Ark moved forward, Moses said, 'Arise, O Lord, and let thine enemies be scattered!' " This verse was incorporated into our prayerbook liturgy, but not until the rabbis appended the prophetic verse, "For out of Zion shall go forth the Torah and the Word of the Lord from Jerusalem."

The future of our people is secure so long as we maintain the Covenant. It matters not to God whether He save many or few. To all of you I say, draw strength from the fellowship of colleagues and friends, pour passion if you will into social meliorism, labor ceaselessly for the spiritual well-being of *Am Yisrael*, but, above all, walk resolutely in the vineyards of the Lord. They are ours to tend.

THE ORIGIN AND AUTHORITY OF THE RABBI

This paper will deal with the rabbi and his authority. It is not intended as a definitive scholarly study. It is my purpose merely to present a springboard for discussion. As one who takes pride in the title of rabbi, I shall endeavor to map out in broad strokes the path by which we have come and the direction in which we should move.

* * *

The institution of the rabbinate is a uniquely Jewish contribution to the sociology of religion. The allocation of spiritual authority in biblical times is indicated in the verse from Jeremiah, "Instruction shall not fail from the priest, nor counsel from the wise nor oracle from the prophet."[1] The priest was the divinely ordained intermediary between God and Israel. He was the supervisor of the cult, the custodian and teacher of the law, and the judge who was the authorized interpreter of that law. The prophet was the charismatic and inspired spokesman for God. He proclaimed the ethical and spiritual ideal under the rubric "Thus saith the Lord." Although sometimes in conflict, the authority each claimed was rooted in the divine will.

During the Second Commonwealth the Torah was canonized. Prophecy was deemed to have ceased as a source of authority. During this period the priestly party, the Sadducees, became dominant, and the nation became in a sense a theocracy. This assumption of exclusive authority, however, did not remain unchallenged. As the prophet had challenged the priestly function on the basis of its ritualistic emphasis, the new challenge came from scholars on the basis of its inflexibility. The new party was called the Pharisees. They were perhaps the descendants of the sages of biblical times. During the last half of the Second Commonwealth, priest and scholar functioned simultaneously, sometimes cooperating, sometimes conflicting. The destruction of the Temple marked the end of the priesthood as an authoritative institution. The Sadducees drop out of the picture; the Pharisees take over. It is in this setting that the rabbi emerges.

The new claim to authority was still rooted in God and in His revealed word, the Torah, viewed as the supreme source for the guidance of life in its totality. But the Torah needed expansion and adaptation to changing circumstances. For this, the concept of the oral law was developed. It permitted such adaptation without loss of the conviction of theistic origin.

As Ellis Rivkin has cogently argued, the concept of the oral law was a revolutionary idea. It actually contradicted the Torah, which said, "All this word which I command you, shall you observe to do; you shalt not add thereto, nor diminish from it."[2] It was based on the assumption that a body of oral teaching supplementing the written Torah was given to Moses at Sinai[3] and transmitted by him in a chain of tradition.[4]

15

The scholars became the authoritative interpreters and transmitters of the divine will as expressed in this oral law.[5] In doing so they assumed that they were rediscovering original revelation. "Everything that a diligent student is destined to teach was already spoken to Moses at Sinai."[6] Some talmudic teachers saw the practical incongruity of this thesis. There is tongue in cheek in the familiar story of Moses foreseeing the future and visiting the academy of Rabbi Akiba only to discover that he cannot follow the argument. He is comforted, however, when Akiba, pressed for his source, answers, *Torah l'Moshe mi-Sinai.*[7]

The implicit understanding was that the law came from the Almighty. But in reaching decisions about it the rabbis took the authority from God's hands. Thus two basic principles were simultaneously accepted: *Torah min hashamayim*—"the Torah comes from Heaven," and *Torah lo bashamayim*—"The Torah is no longer in heaven." The source is divine but its development is in the life of society and the judgment of man. We see this in the famous story of the controversy between Rabbi Eliezer and Rabbi Joshua. God was required to accept the view of the majority, whose authority transcended even that of divine miracles and the Bat Kol itself. In a spirit of parental pride and resignation God said, "My children have vanquished Me."[8]

The title rabbi as a designation for these scholars came into use only after the destruction of the Temple. Previously the word was used to indicate an outstanding person in any field. In the New Testament it is apparently used simply as a mark of respect. As an official title, however, it was first used in reference to Gamaliel, the Nasi and President of the Sanhedrin in the last decades before the destruction, who was called rabban. It was first conferred by Jochanan ben Zakkai upon his disciples.

Semicha was the formal bestowal of that title, continuing a tradition said to have been started by Moses. He had laid his hands upon Joshua, in accordance with God's commandment, that the children of Israel might recognize his claim to leadership.[9] The ceremony now acknowledged mastery of the oral law and the qualification to sit in the Sanhedrin and adjudicate on the basis of that law.

Semicha had no mystical power to confer authority. It was rather evidence of authority. It was *reshut*—carrying the privilege of teaching and judging, transmitted by an acknowledged teacher to his disciple.[10] Ordination in Palestine was later placed in the hands of the Nasi and the rabbis of his academy. A modified ordination was practiced in Babylonia, carrying the title rab. There is some scholarly dispute about when formal ordination ceased, but the formal recognition of those qualified to teach and to judge on the basis of the written and oral law was henceforth an accepted practice. Thus the scholars and judges of each generation were able to claim a line of succession that reached back to Moses. "Whoever is appointed leader of the community, even the least worthy, is to be regarded with the same esteem as the mightiest of earlier generations."[11] "You must hearken to the words of the sages, even if they tell you left is right and right is left; whoever the judge may be, good or bad, has the same authority as Moses."[12]

There were, however, various challenges to this rabbinic authority which are not without contemporary resonances. One was an official challenge from those who served as the secular rulers. In Babylonia this was the exilarch, the Resh Galuta, who manifested the features of a hereditary monarch. He claimed genealogical descent from David. He was recognized as the political leader of the Jewish community by the Sassanian and later by the Moslem government. He collected taxes, exerted control over local communities, and represented Jewry at the royal court. His rule was virtually a state within a state.

Among the powers granted to the exilarchs was that of appointing judges. They welcomed refugee rabbis from Palestine as a source of well-trained officials.[13] A modus vivendi was established, each serving the purposes of the other. The exilarchs represented the Davidic royal tradition, the rabbis represented the Mosaic Torah tradition.[14] The rabbis gave the prestige of scholarly support to the exilarch and received political support from him.

The relationship, however, carried the seeds of potential rivalry and conflict. By the second generation of Amoraim, the rabbis had assumed a level of equality. Semi-annual *kallot* of scholars and laymen were held at the academies. From them the calendar was issued and proclamations made. There, too, the ordination of rabbis was performed. The rivalry reached a climax in the controversy between Saadia Gaon and Exilarch David ben Zakkai in which each sought to depose the other. It was evidenced again in the letter of Samuel ben Ali, a contemporary of the Rambam, who denounced the exilarch as an ignoramus. In this time of exile, he maintained, secular royal power was no longer needed. The authority of the scholars, which could be traced back to Moses himself, should be considered sufficient.[15]

The other challenge to rabbinic authority came from the people themselves. It was expressed in the rights retained by the community and in the power of *minhag*. The Talmud indicates that a religious leader of the community could not be designated without consultation with the community.[16] It was also established that no decree could be issued unless the majority of the community could abide by it.[17]

The power of local custom was particularly significant. *Minhag mevatel halacha*—"Established custom takes precedence over law."[18] The transgression of custom was punishable on the same basis as transgression of the written law. The principle had been accepted that "No *bet din* can abrogate the laws of a previous one unless it is superior in wisdom and numbers."[19] However, if a law is accepted by the large majority of the people, even a superior court cannot abrogate it.[20] When the law was in doubt, common usage served as a guide. *Puk chazi ma ama daber*—"Go out and see what the people say."[21] Again there are two principles. *Minhag avotenu Torah hi*—"The custom of our ancestors is Torah" and *Hakol k'minhag hamedina*—"Everything is according to local custom." Thus both ancient and current custom are authoritative.[22]

Of course there were limits to acceptable custom. In particular, the rabbis tried to safeguard against non-Jewish religious practices. However, even here they were not always totally successful. Where violations of rabbinic edicts were widespread, it was often considered expedient to overlook them. Since our information for this period is derived almost exclusively from rabbinic sources, it may well be that this contradiction between legal enactment and popular practice tends to be understated.

E. R. Goodenough has documented the widespread use of pagan decorative symbols, in spite of the opposition by the Tannaim and Amoraim, in the Greco-Roman period after the middle of the second century.[23] Neusner emphasizes this deviation with reference to the synagogue wall paintings of Dura-Europos and the incantation texts found at Nippur.[24] The same trend is evident in the burial chambers at Bet Shearim and the mosaics in the Galilee synagogues. A recent article in the *Biblical Archaeological Review* on Jewish catacombs of Rome points out that "These decorations . . . reflect how thoroughly some Roman Jews had assimilated Roman culture. The pagan symbolism seemed to belie that these were Jewish catacombs."[25] Thus the customs of the surrounding society had a significant impact on the daily life of the people, resulting in sometimes startling departures from rabbinic teaching.

The rabbis tried to incorporate expressions of respect for their calling into the fabric of social life. Students were to honor their teachers more than their fathers. Every Jew was obligated to rise before a scholar, however youthful. The authority of the scholars, however, was not uncontested and was primarily confined to religious matters. It is told that Rabbi Joseph had to choose between two contenders for a seat on a Babylonian community council. To the rabbi he assigned "affairs relating to heaven." To the other, who was devoid of learning or lineage, he assigned the "affairs of the town."[26]

* * *

Our focus now moves on to the period of the Middle Ages and the Renaissance. With the decline of the Babylonian academies in the tenth and eleventh centuries, there was a period of confusion in Jewish life. We experience one of the periodic shifting of centers which marks the flow of Jewish history. The European Jewish communities found themselves cut off from their source of direction, with no central authority. This encouraged a tendency toward community self-determination. This trend was particularly evident in the Italian communities and later in the Rhineland. These areas followed the Palestinian pattern of local authority rather than the Babylonian pattern of centralized power. By the time distinguished academies had been established whose reputation gave them widespread acceptance on the European scene, local communities had already had centuries of experience in self-government.[27]

Although life was still dominated theoretically by talmudic law, this local independence, coupled with lay leadership, often allowed modification in civil and criminal matters in the light of practical considerations. The judicial system was in the hands of laymen. They often reached their decisions on the basis of common sense. Experts were needed, however, in the areas of ritual and liturgy. And this period developed a new pattern for the rabbinic role—that of the *rab ha-ir*, the communal rabbi.

According to the testimony of Judah ben Barzilai of Barcelona, in order to designate a rabbi in this period it became customary to issue a *ketab masmich*, a writ of ordination, which marked the recipient as rabbi or rab or haham.[28] This was different, however, from the ancient Palestinian *semicha*. It involved no laying on of hands. And most significantly, it could be conferred by the city elders or the synagogue elders. The diploma acknowledged learning and qualifications to act as *dayan*. However, it did not confer any authority beyond that which the community was willing to bestow in the light of the recipient's scholarly reputation.

After the Black Death in the middle of the fourteenth century there was another period of confusion and intellectual decay. Often illiterate men were inducted into rabbinical office. Again the need was felt for formal and more demanding standards. In 1370 Meir ben Baruch Halevi of Vienna issued an ordinance requiring that a rabbi be authorized by another rabbi of standing who would confer on him the title of Morenu. It was a testimonial of his fitness to interpret halacha.[29]

Bearers of these titles were eligible for the new office of *rab ha-ir*. They were primarily instructors and preachers and ritual experts. The element of innovation lay in the fact that it was based on a contractual relationship. The *ketav rabbanut* specified privileges, duties, and rights. Rab was now the designation of a community officeholder.

A typical *ketav rabbanut* during this period described the qualities of the rabbi with standardized *melitza* and exaggerated praise. Power, however, was often severely limited. In many cases the issue of *takkanot* required the consent of the *kahal*. The rabbi's right to use the ban as an enforcement of decisions was dependent on community approval. He was required to issue *gezerot* when requested by the *parnassim*. In some communities the attempt was made to subject rabbis to taxes from which they had previously been exempt. Under any circumstances the rabbi's authority applied only to the community that had appointed him. In Venice in 1614 the rabbi was forbidden to ordain except with the approval of the lay leaders. In 1628 they usurped the right to impose the ban without consultation with the rabbi. In Florence the community dispensed altogether with the services of a rabbi, and lay leaders administered the law even in matrimonial affairs.[30] In general, the non-rabbinical courts dealt with civil and financial matters while the rabbi was assigned the supervision of *dat vadin*, religious and ritual matters.[31]

Once again we have a situation with potential conflict. Again there is the competition with secular officials. Courtiers exerted considerable influence in Jewish affairs. In the tenth century, for example, in Cordova, the approval of Hasdai ibn Shaprut, who we know was a generous patron of Jewish learning, was required for the appointment of a rabbi-judge. Many such courtiers, however, were reluctant to share their power with the rabbis. The Nasi Sheshet Isaac ben Benveniste in Castile in the latter part of the twelfth century, for example, criticized rabbis who opposed Rambam's *Mishneh Torah*. He indicated that they were concerned that their monopoly on legal interpretation might be undermined. He favored the code because in his view it simplified the law so that ordinary laymen could dispense with rabbinical guidance and make decisions themselves.[32]

A new element entered the situation with the completion of the professionalization of the rabbinate in the fourteenth and fifteenth centuries, when the payment of salaries to the community rabbis became common. The main tension now was in relation to the *parnassim* upon whom the rabbis were dependent for their livelihood.

It must be admitted that the pressure for material security tempted some rabbis to overlook moral principles and responsibilites.[33] In the thirteenth century criticisms of low ethical standards on the part of certain rabbis were common. One writer charged them with using their talmudic knowledge and techniques for dishonest financial benefit in cases in which they themselves were involved. As Israel Bettan has shown, Ephraim Luntschitz in the sixteenth century and Jonathan Eybeschutz in the eighteenth denounced rabbis who concentrated on prayer and ritual and refrained from grappling with moral evils that disrupted society. They charged that such themes were avoided in order not to antagonize the wealthy lay leaders who were all too often among those guilty. It was for this reason, they concluded, that preachers were held in contempt.[34]

In Italy in the meantime two kinds of *semicha* had developed. There was *semicha merabanut*, which carried the title *morenu harav*, and *semicha mehaberut*, with the title *haver*. Only the first was authorized to teach *halacha l'maase*.[35] But perhaps under the influence of the surrounding Catholic society, the rabbinate tended to be given a more sacerdotal and clerical posture.

Rabbis were often greatly concerned about their personal prestige. In one case in Italy an unsuccessful effort was made to establish the principle that the rabbi should be called to the Torah before an unlearned kohen.[36] Sometimes the rabbi took for himself high-sounding titles like *manhig* and *rosh gola*. These titles, however, usually reflect not reality but a measure of insecurity. In communal administration it was the *parnassim* who had the power, and rabbis were limited largely to *dat vadin*.[37] For those unwilling to compromise, the situation was ripe for conflict.

The struggle against lay encroachment is reflected in the attack of Leon de Modena of Venice in 1630 against the communal prohibition of gambling under penalty of *herem*. One of the strongest grounds of his argument was the failure of the secular leaders to consult rabbinic scholars, without which no *herem* should be imposed. In matters of religious law, he insisted, the congregation must live under rabbinic direction. He concluded, therefore, that the decree had no validity.[38]

Occasionally we hear echoes that have come to be quite familiar. In the introduction to a manuscript translation of the Tanach into Yiddish-German in 1510 we read that if a rabbi studies day and night and does not wish to engage in small talk with his *baalebatim*, they will say, "Let's get another rabbi who won't despise our conversation."[39] Balancing this is the controversy over tenure between the community of Vilna and Rabbi Samuel. Among other things he was charged with spending insufficient time at his books. Witnesses testified that many times there was no light in his study after midnight.[40]

The Maharal of Prague, who died in 1609, poses the problem in his *Netivot Olam*. "Woe to us that the rabbi is dependent on the heads of the community— that every year or every three years his appointment is reviewed. And how should he not fear, since he is in their power, conscious of the possibility that they may not renew his contract?"[41]

Compensation for rabbis was not usually munificent. One contract, however, may evoke our envy. In 1539 in Verona the *ketav haminui* of Rabbi Yitzchak of

Latash stated that the purpose of his appointment was to assure *limud Torah* in the community. His duty was to teach one *pesak* every day between morning prayers and breakfast, and the rest of the day, it specifically stated, was for his own pleasure and welfare and he was free and his own master. For this he was paid 100 escudos annually and a fine residence, befitting his *kovod, b'chinam.* This, however, was for the position of rosh yeshiva. The *rav ha-ir* usually did not do nearly so well. In the contract of Todros of Friedberg in 1575, however, it was specifically provided that among his perquisites was the privilege of eating and drinking at a *seudat mitzvah* like *brit milah* or *nisuin, b'chinam.* That apparently was to compensate him for the fact that it was also specified that he could not change the *minhagim* of the community without the permission of the *chevruta.*[42]

There were, of course, contradictory trends. The rabbi's theoretical position in the community was central, and where one had scholarly competence and a strong personality, he might very well be accepted as the acknowledged leader of Jewish life. Baron cites the heyday of rabbinic power and influence in Germany from the fifteenth to the seventeenth century and in Eastern Poland in the nineteenth, when the rabbi wielded almost unchallenged power. In Eastern Europe, for example, rabbinic tenure became law. Moses Sofer could say, "No one ever heard or saw in these lands that a rabbi should be deposed, and one ought never to do such a thing."[43] A unique situation developed in the Chasidic movement, which began as a rebellion against the rigid authority of law and ended as acceptance of the absolute authority of the tzaddik. But in general we find the rabbi in the difficult and paradoxical position of one who must maintain his integrity when employed by people he sought to lead.

*   *   *

The Emancipation introduced a totally new dimension in Jewish life and in the role of the rabbi. Jews had to adapt to a fundamentally changed social pattern. In the ancient and medieval periods Jewish life had been all-embracing. Persian monarchs, Moslem caliphs, and Christian princes had granted Jews virtually complete internal autonomy, including jurisdiction over both religious and what we call secular matters. Now this semi-autonomous status disintegrated. As Jews entered into the stream of general society, Jewish life became more restricted. Many Jews were now striving to live in two worlds; on the one hand to adapt to the pattern of contemporary life, on the other to remain Jewish. At the same time the reevaluation of the sacred in the value system of Judaism in the light of science, democracy, and freedom of thought made the old standards of authority based on divine sanctions no longer applicable.

The role of the rabbinical scholar was now radically altered. He lost much of his influence, and many of his functions were changed. It was in this setting that Reform Judaism emerged. It was begun by laymen stressing practical modifications. Rabbis at first attempted to defend change on the basis of traditional interpretation. This was doomed to failure because the infallible character of traditional law was no longer operative. Reform represented a revolt not only against the interpretation of the law but against the whole basis of its authority. As our late beloved colleague Bernard Bamberger has said, "You cannot use authority to justify the rejection of that authority. Tradition might sanction reforms—it could not sanction Reform."[44]

This new approach, which negated the unique authority of rabbinical interpretation, complicated the rabbinic role. Reform rabbis themselves contributed to this. In the battle over the Hamburg Prayerbook Aaron Horin said, "We are far from making necessary reforms dependent on the approval of every rabbinic authority. . . . In a formal rabbinism we see a hierarchic authority which we reject as error." Frankel, the leader of positive-historical Judaism, from which Conservative Judaism was to emerge, said, "There are no clergymen who by higher inspiration stand above the laymen; but only teachers, who expound the Law."[45] Geiger maintained that "Neither as priest, by his ordination, nor as officer, by the material power of the state, is he entitled to interfere in the direction of religious affairs; but only through his knowledge."[46]

On the other hand the dangers of uncontrolled revolutionary change by laymen was highlighted in the extreme Declaration of Principles issued in 1842 by the Frankfurt Society of friends of Reform who felt no need for rabbinical guidance. In it, among other radical changes, the rite of circumcision was declared no longer binding. It stimulated Reform rabbis to assume leadership in a more positive direction.

This confrontation was intensified when the center of Reform Judaism was transferred to the new world. For here the community structure of European Jewry was replaced by the synagogue-centered structure of American Jewish life. In this setting the authority of the rabbi was posed against the power of the synagogue.

The problem of rabbinic authority versus congregational autonomy emerged at the second conference of the CCAR in 1891. Interestingly it was associated with an issue which still vexes us, *milat gerim*. It was launched with an open letter from Henry Berkowitz, who submitted the problem, as he said, "to the rabbis in whom are vested the authority and duty to decide all such matters . . ."[47]

The response was given by Rabbi Felsenthal of Chicago. "Have you or I or any other Reform rabbi that right and authority? . . . I disclaim any authority and protest against the arrogant assumption of ecclesiastical authority by any rabbi or by any number of rabbis." Thus he vehemently supports the authority of the individual autonomous congregation as opposed to either individual rabbis or a synod of rabbis.[48] Emil G. Hirsch further developed this position. "Rabbis have not the right to presume today to set their authority as rabbis, if there be such a thing in Judaism, against the discussion of this or any other question by whomsoever. There is no distinction in Judaism between layman and clergyman. There is only one between the scholar and the nonscholar."[49]

A different approach was taken by Isaac M. Wise who, from the beginning of the CCAR, stressed the Conference as the source and safeguard of rabbinic authority. He was convinced that the actions and resolutions of this body could serve as the standards of Jewish practice. "It is the duty of the united rabbis to protect Judaism from stagnation and each individual rabbi from attack. . . . All reforms ought to go into practice on the authority of the Conference. . . . If many support one, one is a power. If one sustains many, he acquires the wisdom and energy of the many. We must have a united rabbinate."[50]

Wise retuned to this theme two years later, reiterating the power and purpose of the Conference: "Reform represented the popular spirit in producing new customs and observances. But it had become anarchical until the Conference and synods of the last half century which turned the new spirit into legitimate channels."[51]

The conflict over rabbinical authority on the American scene came into further focus in the issue of freedom of the pulpit. Isaac M. Wise himself confronted this problem in the historic incident in Albany when physical violence was used to prevent his use of the pulpit. Some years later he was again involved in this issue when he was invited by Leo Merzbacher of Temple Emanu-El in New York as a guest preacher. The Board then adopted a resolution that no one could occupy the pulpit without its permission. At Mikveh Israel in Philadelphia, Isaac Leeser was instructed: "The cantor must present a copy of any speech or sermon to the Board of Trustees and receive their permission to deliver it." He was furthermore prohibited from making any announcement except the time of worship. Rabbi Gustav Gottheil of Emanu-El was required to apologize to the Board for having objected to the excessive interference by the president in the religious school. It was again in connection with Emanu-El that the classic case involving Stephen S. Wise occurred in which the principle of pulpit freedom was made a public issue. [52]

As time passed and the Reform movement in America became established and lost its revolutionary spirit, a new, somewhat unhealthy trend manifested itself in the matter of rabbinic authority. While laymen maintained their leadership and authority in temple administration, in religious matters the rabbi took over not so much by qualification as by default. Massive Jewish illiteracy on the part of the membership made him the custodian of Jewish knowledge, and widespread disinterest made him the proxy for Jewish observance. Decisions about religious practices were left in his hands without question, provided he was not too demanding. In their concern with social problems and the implementation of the social ideals of religion, rabbis were usually far ahead of their laymen, who looked upon their spiritual leaders as naive idealists.

In the last few decades there has been a needed reversal in this trend. Such reversal, however, carries its own dangers. The official policy of the Union of American Hebrew Congregations has been toward increased lay participation in all areas of religious life. This has been particularly marked and stimulated by the inventiveness and creativity of our youth movement. Let me say that the spirit, the commitment, and the involvement of the best of our young people today is far beyond anything one could have imagined when I began my rabbinical service. The danger in that involvement is that it sometimes becomes an end in itself, with the blind leading the blind. Granted the implementation of Judaism was never intended to become the sole prerogative of the rabbi. But on the other hand the rabbi cannot be dispensed with, without disastrous consequences. We still must work out the proper constructive relationship between the roles of rabbi and layman.

* * *

Let me now summarize where we have come. My analysis has indicated first that the unique and unquestioned power and prestige of the rabbinic office in former days which has generally been assumed is not substantiated by the literature or historical sources. The struggle for power between rabbi and laymen is a continuous element of Jewish social history. The story of the rabbi in the past as in the present is one of tension and conflict, of struggle and searching to find and fulfill his role. And that role has usually been most effective when it involved specialization in religious leadership.

Second, through most of our history the rabbinic office carried no coercive power in and of itself. Rabbinic law was normative law, and the rabbi assumed his authority not because of his office but because of his mastery of this law. The people accepted it as a divinely sanctioned obligation. His authority lay in his scholarly attainments and in the corresponding measure of his acceptance by the community.

Third, in the contemporary world rabbinic authority is no longer backed by the sanction of divine origin. The element of compulsion and coercion has been eliminated. The stress is now totally on voluntary acceptance. As sociologists have put it, our authority is no longer imperative, it is now influential.[53]

In what direction, then, shall we proceed? How can we most effectively function as rabbis? In what way can our authority be manifested today? We live in a radically different world than our colleagues of previous generations. But the historic patterns still apply.

First, scholarly qualifications still remain the basis for the authority of the contemporary rabbi. But the character of that scholarship differs from that inherent in our historic tradition. No longer does it imply mastery of the halacha, which carries no compulsion for the liberal Jew. We cannot compel acceptance of our recommendations with quotations from the Bible or Talmud. We cannot enforce our values by threats of punishment. Even the force of public opinion is no longer effective. Not that halacha can be ignored. But halacha for us is the beginning, not the end. In Freehof's terms it must be for guidance, not for governance. And so halachic mastery, which was the desired standard if not always the actual competence of the traditional rabbi, is no longer expected of, and need no longer be striven for by, the contemporary Reform rabbi.

Nor does scholarly qualification stress, as it did for several generations, the ability to transmit general culture. During the period of adjustment to the new world the Reform rabbi was often one of the tiny elite who had had the privilege of advanced academic studies. It was part of his role to share with his less-advantaged people something of the perspective of literature, history, and modern science that would broaden their outlook. Today many members of our congregations are our equals or superiors in these areas.

Torah for the modern Jew must be not halacha alone but the total spectrum of Jewish values. It incorporates the unique perspective of the Jewish heritage.

From this context the rabbi must be able to deal with the problems of life and society. He is the expert in Judaism. His understanding of Jewish history, literature, philosophy—his involvement in Jewish liturgy, and observance and life—must all be brought to bear in his guidance of synagogue activities, in his interpretation of Judaism, and in his views of society.[54]

Secondly, more than ever the authority of the contemporary rabbi depends upon congregational acceptance. The rabbi is a teacher who communicates knowledge which the student can either accept or reject. It is not enough that he be an expert in Jewish knowledge. Somehow he must transmit to his congregation respect for its values. Many lectures and sermons in our *CCAR Yearbooks* have dealt with this recurrent theme. And again and again we find the thesis that rabbinical influence and authority depend on the quality and impact of the individual personality.

Typical of them is the statement of Jacob Rudin in a discussion on this subject some years ago: "The rabbi is no longer defined as the expounder of the law. His authority derives not from scholarly competence but from his own attibutes of personality. The Reform rabbi whose word and deed have won him the confidence of his congregation wields authority in his congregation."[55]

By personality I do not mean the possession of charisma and charm. What I mean is the sincerity and commitment, the caring ministry, which earn respect and admiration, yes, and affection and loyalty from the congregation.

In his study of the rabbi and the synagogue Lenn stresses that it is this quality in the rabbi which is the psychological component of a synagogue's willingness to accept change.[56] Conservative rabbis in their journal have stressed the same idea.[57] And I would add to them my personal testimony based on almost half a century of congregational experience.

Thirdly, there must be a new emphasis upon the role of the layman in Jewish life. This applies in all branches of Judaism. The late Rabbi Samuel Belkin of Yeshiva University wrote, "So much of the law involves policies in which the laity may be equally or even more knowledgeable, the decision-making process should not be by rabbis alone."[58] In the *Proceedings of the Rabbinical Assembly* a Conservative rabbi is quoted: "Leaders must be those capable of wielding power. . . . But the laity which leads the Jewish community is devoid of knowledge or spiritual values. The rabbi's role is to teach them."

Lay leadership in community affairs is a common pattern of reality which rabbis often complain about but cannot reverse. Sometimes our laymen are ahead of rabbis in social consciousness. Lay participation in religious activities is no longer a rarity. This does not diminish the importance of the rabbinic role. Rather it enhances it. For the lay participation is rarely Jewish in character. The rabbi must stress the Jewish dimension and spiritual values in synagogue and community affairs. He must educate his laymen so that their involvement will be an authentic one.

Let us not be too distressed, then, if laymen and secular organizations play an active role in the civil concerns of Jewish life, in fund-raising and distribution, in defense activity, in political action. Let us not be troubled if they are not satisfied to allow the rabbinate to stand alone in social action but are ready to move ahead with us. In these areas of life, the rabbi in our times as through all the ages must take his place as *primus inter pares*—first among equals. The measure of authority he will wield, the degree of leadership he will occupy, will be determined by his individual qualifications. His title of rabbi gives him no greater claim to a central position than any other Jew. But in religious matters he is the teacher and the specialist. Here too he must be prepared to work side by side with laymen. But as a rabbi he must have the qualification through education and character which warrants his leadership and which will evoke the willingness on the part of laymen to be guided by him.

The problems remain, among them:

What part does faith play in the rabbi's scholarly armor that makes him different from a secular professor of Jewish studies whose academic expertise may be equal or greater?

How will the impact of the rabbi be affected as a growing percentage of our colleagues are involved in non-congregational assignments?

How does the rabbi's moral influence enter into a society where moral standards are in flux, particularly in the area of sexuality, at a time when it is considered bad form to make moral judgments?

How can the rabbi protect himself from becoming a routine invocator, a formal but ineffectual appendage in Jewish public affairs?

How can he exert his influence on powerful laymen who feel no need for rabbinical guidance or Jewish authenticity?

What role can the Conference play as source or bulwark of rabbinic authority?

One thing we can be sure of—the rabbi's role will not be strengthened if he looks upon it as a purely professional one in which compensation is received for services rendered. Lenn's study indicates that most congregants view their rabbi as the dispenser of professional services. If we are only that, the time may come when there will be all too few who will require these services. Yes, we are professionals in the sense that we earn our livelihood from our labors. But in our understandable concern about the hard material realities of our position and the financial security of our families, about salaries and contracts, tenure and pensions, we must never forget that ours is an historic calling of learning and spiritual leadership and moral idealism. To our people we must be the examples and the teachers. It is not our task to monopolize the leadership of the Jewish community but to give it direction and purpose. There could be no more challenging task or nobler calling.

NOTES

1. Jer. 18:18.
2. Deut. 13:1.
3. Meg. 19b; Ber. 5a.
4. Avot 1:1.
5. Deut. 17:9-12. Here it is indicated that in the future "You shall appear before the magistrate in charge at the time." The key words are "at the time."
6. Peah 17a.
7. Menachot 29b.
8. B.M. 59b.
9. Num. 27:18f. In Jewish tradition Moses himself was given a kind of honorary ordination with the designation, Moshe Rabbenu.

10. Sanhedrin 5b.

11. Rosh Hashana 25b.

12. Sifri to Deut. 17:11.

13. Neusner, Jacob, *There We Sat Down*, Nashville, 1972.

14. Ibid., p. 59.

15. Asaf, Simcha, "Igrot R. Shmuel," in *Tarbitz I*, 1930, pp. 65-66.

16. Ber. 55a. This was the basis of an edict issued in the twelfth century by Rashbam, Rabbenu Tam, and 150 other sages, later cited by the Chatam Sofer in the nineteenth century. Responsa #19.

17. B.B. 60b; A.Z. 36a.

18. It is to be noted that this source indicates that *minhag* always anticipates halacha. However a *minhag* that has no evidence in the Torah is to be considered like an error in legal judgment.

19. Eduyot 1:5.

20. A.Z. 36a.

21. Berachot 45a.

22. Heller, Bernard, *CCAR Yearbrook*, 1951.

23. Goodenough, Erwin R., "Rabbis and Jewish Art in the Greco-Roman Period," *HUCA #32*, pp. 269-279.

24. Neusner, Jacob, prev. cit., p. 14.

25. Petigliani, Letizia, in *BAR*, Vol. 6, #3, May-June 1980, p. 43.

26. Kidd. 26b

27. Baron, Salo, *The Jewish Community*, Vol. II, p. 69.

28. Ibid., Vol. II, pp. 67-68.

29. Ibid., Vol. II, p. 90.

30. Ibid., Vol. II, p. 77.

31. Breuer, Mordechai, *Rabbanut Ashkenaz b'yeme Habenayim*, Jerusalem, 1976, p. 14.

32. Marx, Alexander, "Texts by and About Maimonides," *JQR* XXV, 1934-5, p. 427. Cf. Silver, Daniel J., *Maimonidean Criticism and Maimonidean Controversy, 1180-1240*. (Leiden, 1965), p. 129, Note 3.

33. Baron, S., prev. cit. Vol. II, p. 87. Breuer, M., prev. cit., p. 24. See discussion by Marc Saperstein, *Decoding the Rabbis*, Cambridge, 1979, pp. 177-179.

34. Bettan, Israel, *Studies in Jewish Preaching*, Cincinnati, 1939, p. 287 and pp. 328-9.

35. Bonfil, Reuben, *Harabanut b'Italya bitekufat ha-Renascence*, Jerusalem, 1979, p. 27.

36. Ibid., p. 54.

37. Breuer, M., prev. cit. p. 25.

38. Naveh, P., Ed., Modena, Leon Judah, "Zikne Yehuda" in *Leket Ketavim*, Jerusalem, 1968, pp. 181-2.

39. Breuer, M., prev. cit., p. 116.

40. Baron S., prev. cit., Vol. II, p. 86.

41. Breuer, prev. cit., p. 118.

42. Bonfil R., prev. cit., p. 69.

43. Baron S., prev. cit., Vol. II, p. 88.

44. Bamberger, Bernard, *The Story of Judaism*, New York, 1964, pp. 279ff.

45. Jewish Encyclopedia, Vol. X, p. 296.

46. Ibid.

47. *CCAR Yearbook*, Vol. II, 1891, p. 85.

48. Ibid., pp. 86ff.

49. Ibid., p. 128.

50. *CCAR Yearbook*, Vol. I, 1890, p. 19.

51. *CCAR Yearbook*, Vol. III, 1892, p. 9.

52. Wise, Stephen S., *Challenging Years*, pp. 82ff.

53. Carlin, Jerome E. and Mendlovitz, Saul H., "The American Rabbi: A Religious Specialist Reponds to Loss of Authority," in *The Jews*, Marshall Sklare, ed., Glencoe, Ill., 1958, pp. 375ff.

54. Saperstein, H., "Changing Role of the Rabbi," in *The American Rabbi*, New York, 1977, p. 163.

55. *CCAR Journal*, Oct., 1962.

56. Lenn, Theodore I., *Rabbi and Synagogue in Reform Judaism*, 1972, pp. 297ff.

57. Karp, Abraham J., "Rabbi, Congregation and the World They Live in," *Conservative Judaism*, Vol. 26, #1, Fall 1971.

58. Quoted by Rabbi Emanuel Rackman in *Jewish Week*, December 23-30, 1979.

RABBINIC AUTHORITY: ARTICLES AND PAPERS

THE SOURCE OF REFORM HALACHIC AUTHORITY

Walter Jacob

We can, as we have gathered from the paper of my honored colleague, Dr. Harold Saperstein, look at the entire question of authority in the rabbinate in its broadest or narrowest framework. A broad framework would include a discussion of the authority of religion in general, its status in the modern world, the status of religious Judaism versus ethnic or national forms of Judaism, the role of the synagogue in modern Jewish life, the role of Israel, and the perennial struggle between the rabbinate and the laity. Each of these matters and a number of others deserve our attention. Let me, however, concentrate on a specific area. If, after everything else has been settled, some rabbinic authority remains, what is its underlying Jewish basis within the tradition and within Reform Jewish tradition? It is my premise that the bases for traditional Jewish authority and liberal Jewish authority are rather similar. They are nearer to each other than we and traditionalists are likely to admit.

The source of Judaism's authority lies in the word of God; Judaism has based itself on a combination of the written law (*Torah shebichtav*) and the oral law (*Torah sheba-al peh*) (Meg. 19b); the latter contains all the enactments of the Talmud which are not specifically mentioned in the Bible. The chain of tradition became clear to the authorities of the Mishnah and the Talmud and is recorded at the beginning of the Pirke Avot (M. Avot 1:1). When faced with the many changes made by later scholars, the tradition stated that Moses had received the principles of the law and that all the particulars were really included in them, left open to later interpretation (Ex.R. 41:6). Though the law in its totality was of divine origin, once it had been given into human hands it was up to the scholars of a given period to make the proper decisions, and no further divine interference was to play any role. So, in a discussion between Rabbi Eliezer ben Hyrkanos and Rabbi Joshua ben Hananiah, the latter's opinion was declared correct because a majority followed him, although a heavenly voice (*bat kol*) intervened in behalf of the former's opinion (B.M. 59b; similarly Ber. 52a; Pes. 114a). Legal logic (*savarah*) was, therefore, an acknowledged source of law (Git. 6b; Shab. 63a). We can see, therefore, that by the talmudic period direct divine revelation had been replaced by human authority and by the traditions created through the centuries. This, then, was a vast change from the biblical period.

When there is a conflict in the Talmud between an earlier authority and a later authority, the earlier authority's decision is decisive, so the Amoraim were not permitted to dispute a decision of the Tannaim (Er. 53a). If scholars were of an equal status and a rabbinical decree was involved, then one was free to choose the more lenient decision though the stricter view was adopted when dealing with a biblical injunction (A.Z. 7a). Scholars should always be careful of their colleagues' opinions and not permit what they have prohibited or prohibit what they have permitted (Ber. 63b; Nidah 20b). Yet, if a scholar felt that he was more capable than his colleagues, he might render a totally different decision (Hul. 49a). There are sets of rules which govern conflicting decisions of scholars in the mishnaic, talmudic (for some discussion see A.Z. 7a), and geonic periods; these have been used by the later codes in order to present clear sets of regulations. We can, therefore, see that even in the talmudic period, in which the Jewish communities with which we are concerned lived in relatively close proximity in Babylon and Israel, conflicting traditions developed. There was no longer one tradition, but several traditions. Sometimes it was possible to make a clear decision or to find a compromise. On other occasions, several traditions continued side by side through the centuries.

In order to maintain a measure of freedom and to enable scholars of later periods to render decisions applicable to their own time, a different principle was evolved in the geonic period. This rule (*Hilcheta Kevatra-ei*) stated that the law followed the latest *halachic* authority; Asher ben Yehiel stated this was logical, as the later scholars not only knew the opinions and background of the earlier rabbis, but were able to add their own insights (Asher ben Yehiel, *Piskei Harosh* to B.M. 3:10; 4:21: San. 4:6; *Responsa Rosh* 55.9; see also *Responsa Maharik* 84 [Joseph Colon]; Isserles to *Shulhan Aruch*, Hoshen Mishpat 25:2).This held true even if a student dissented from his teacher (Responsa Maharik 84) or if one scholar disagreed with several earlier scholars (*Pithei T'shuvah* 8 to *Shulhan Aruch*, Hoshen Mishpat 25). This was the line of reasoning accepted by the *Shulhan Aruch* (Isserles to *Shulhan Aruch*, Hoshen Mishpat 25:2); it provided authority along with flexibility in interpreting the divine written and oral law. Whatever inflexibility remained in the Talmud's latest strata was, therefore, removed by the Geonim and subsequent development.

Another line of authority extended through the legislative actions of a rabbinic court (*bet din*) through ordinances (*g'zerot* and *takanot*). The authority to initiate legislation was derived from Deuteronomy: "According to the law which they shall teach thee and according to the judgment which they shall tell thee, thou shalt do" (Deut 17:11); "Ask thy father and he will declare unto thee; thine elders, and they will tell thee" (Deut 32:7). The Mishnah restricted the power of a rabbinic court through the statement that one *bet din* could not overrule the ordinance of another unless it exceeded it in wisdom and number (Eduyot 1:5). The statement proved to be less restrictive than it appears, as the original *bet din* could include a clause saying that its decision could be annulled by a later court (Moed Katan 3b; also Tos. to Baba Kama 82b). Furthermore, if a decision was simply not accepted by the people, then a later court was able to annul it (*Yad*, Hil. Mamrim 2:7). An element of democracy clearly existed from the mishnaic period onward, and the voice of the people played a major role in both legal decisions and custom. A decision could also be invalidated if the original reason for the law was no longer valid (Betzah 5a, b; Rabad on *Yad*, Hil. Mamrim 2:2). In an emergency, a *bet din* which did not consider itself equal to an earlier court could also annul its decisions (*Yad*, Hil. Mamrim 2:4). The *bet din's takanot* represented an extension of divine authority.

Another line of authority came from actual legal decisions rendered by a *bet din* or an individual scholar in reponsa; the precedent (*ma-aseh*) thus created served as an important source from very early times (B.B. 10:8; Shab. 24:5; *Jerushalmi* Ber. 2c). This was possible in keeping with the principle that the Torah had been given into human hands and it was man's duty to interpret it (B.M. 59b). Scholars were cautioned to exercise great care in their decisions, which formed a new line of authority (Ber. 11a; Tosefta, Ber. 1:6), and there should be a general understanding that a decision was intended for practical guidance (B.B. 130b). Precedent (*ma-aseh*) was, however, not considered to be binding, so a judge could even decide a similar case differently if he now saw matters differently (*Ran* and *Ritba* to B.B. 130b; Elon, *Hamishpat Haivri*, pp. 795ff). The responsa literature thus forms an enormous body of precedent which possesses authority. The responsa written in many lands therefore created additional diversity. The Jewish communities were often not in contact with each other or only intermittently, so therefore the local authorities became decisive. We can see very clearly that many different lines of reasoning developed. This was true on major matters like the question of who is a Jew, which had to be dealt with in connection with the Marranos, and a variety of totally conflicting opinions were given through the centuries. It was also true in many minor matters. Hundreds of examples could be given.

Aside from authority which functioned directly through the rabbis as religious leaders, there was the strong authority of popular consensus expressed through custom (*minhag*); this was recognized from early times (Ber. 45a; Pes. 54a). It too provided a vague tie to divine tradition and was legitimized through the statement of Hillel: "Leave it to Israel; if they are not prophets, they are yet the children of prophets" (Pes. 66a). Some biblical passages were also cited: "Thou shalt not remove thy neighbor's landmark, which they have set of olden times" (Deut 19:14); "Hear, my son, the instruction of thy father, and forsake not the teaching of thy mother" (Prov 1:8). The principle of custom overriding the law (*minhag m'vatel halachah*) was restricted to civil law (Solomon b. Simon Duran, *Responsa* 562; Hul. 63a; B.M. 69b); other restrictions were placed upon local customs and customs which were unreasonable or in error. Isserles demonstrated the importance of custom (*minhag*) as a source of authority by recording hundreds of them in his notes to the *Shulhan Aruch:* he stated that "The custom of our fathers is a law *(Torah)*" (*Shulhan Aruch*, Orah Hayyim 690:17; Yoreh Deah 376:4). Perhaps the greatest diversity always existed in matters of custom. There, even the customs of local communities or congregations within a large city were respected, no matter how different they might have been.

Authority for traditional Judaism was divine and was transmitted through human interpretation, legislation, precedent, and custom. The line of authority became diffuse as soon as the Diaspora extended beyond Babylonia. Attempts were made to centralize authority: among the most notable was the effort of Jacob Berab (1474-1546) to reestablish rabbinic ordination (*semichah*) and, thereby, a centralized *bet din* which could act as a court of ultimate authority, but his efforts did not bear fruit. More successful were the various legal codes which sought to provide authoritative, clear decisions in every area of Jewish concern; Maimonides' *Mishneh Torah* and Caro's *Shulhan Aruch* were the most notable examples of this effort at centralized authority.

None of these efforts came anywhere near success; the local rabbi and his congregation always possessed a considerable degree of autonomy. If, in a responsum, he could show authority for a decision which varied from some of the codes, then that might well be accepted. This has been true through the ages.

We have not touched on the crucial problem of enforcement, for only the power to enforce decisions could establish and guarantee authority. In most of the talmudic period, such authority was given either to the Geonate or to the heads of various academies. Presumably, a good deal of such authority continued into the gaonic period. One modern scholar has suggested that the beginnings of the Karaite movement occurred in those communities in which the centralized rabbinic authority could no longer be enforced (Phillip Sigal's *The Emergence of Contemporary Judaism*, Vol. II). In any case, the Karaite movement and its enormous power and influence through the centuries can be seen as a vigorous objection against all centralized authority. In the Middle Ages the power to enforce rules depended on the relationship of the Jewish community with a non-Jewish secular ruler who governed. These conditions changed constantly, and so sometimes a real enforcing power existed; at other times not. Frequently, powerful wealthy individual Jews were able to escape such enforcing powers through the favor of the non-Jewish secular ruler.

In the modern Western world, the only enforcing agency is the will of the community, and as the Jewish community in all Western lands is highly fragmented, one can only speak of rabbinic decisions as guidance even in the most Orthodox setting. Matters are somewhat different in Israel, where family law and certain other items lie within the jurisdiction of the rabbinic courts and their decisions are enforced by the government as law. On the other hand, vast other areas are left to the general courts, and in these matters rabbinic authority is limited to guidance and persuasion.

We should remember that even in traditional Judaism much diversity has always existed and continued nowadays. Efforts on the part of the two chief rabbis of Israel to reach some agreement between themselves have failed, as have efforts to unite even the various Orthodox communities in the United States or in Europe. The questions which are raised have not been minor, but have touched the core of Judaism. Nevertheless, diverse decisions have been given. In addition, of course, traditional Judaism depends upon the will of the people to accept a decision. No enforcement mechanism exists outside of Israel, and there it is limited to a few segments of life. This means that traditional decisions have become "guidance" rather than law.

The pattern which we Reform Jews have followed since the inception of our movement is akin to that of Orthodox Judiasm, but we have stressed diversity, individual freedom, and the ability of the latest generation to interpret and change practices completely if necessary. We have based our decisions on God's revelation in the Bible, in the rabbinic tradition, and to our own leaders.

As Reform Judaism has stressed the individual and the need to make personal decisions in connection with Jewish thought and Jewish practices, so it has also laid a great deal of emphasis on individual freedom. Both the rabbi and the congregation are autonomous, yet in a sense a member, by joining a congregation, signifies acceptance of the authority of the rabbi for guidance and inspiration. The rabbi has also made an implied contract through the ordination which he has received and the rabbinic body which he has decided to join.

Despite this high degree of individualism, we have surrendered authority in another unique direction to conferences and conventions which have played an important part in our religious life since the middle of the last century. In other words, we have channeled the democratic impulse of Judaism into organized efforts. The conferences and synods have brought some uniformity and guidance to the Reform movement. Aaron Chorin (1766-1844), the early Hungarian reformer, felt that centralized authority for the changes sought by the Reform movement should reside in a synod comprising rabbinic and lay leaders, somewhat akin to the Napoleonic Sanhedrin, which was, however, inspired from the outside; he suggested (1831) that such a meeting be arranged. Later, Isaac Mayer Wise (1819-1900) sought to convene a similar body; although there was considerable debate about this matter in the early rabbinic conferences, nothing came of the idea of such a central authoritative body. Abraham Geiger (1810-1874) urged in 1837 that uniform changes be made through rabbinic conferences, and the first conference was held in that year, but nothing substantive was accomplished till the Brunswick Conference of 1844, which was followed by a series of others in Germany and the United States. These meetings have discussed virtually every aspect of Jewish life and made decisions in connection with them. When religious ideas, practices, and customs had lost their meaning, they have willingly or reluctantly acknowledged the fact. Although sometimes antinomian in mood, Reform Judaism has worked within a broad framework of traditional authority. The rabbinic conference held in Brunswick (1844) made decisions about the nature of the service, marriage, divorce, dietary laws, and much else by adapting the past to the present. These decisions were made in the spirit of both the biblical and the rabbinic tradition, but with the clear understanding that the *Shulhan Aruch* was no longer our central guiding authority. That was made absolutely clear through a statement of the Augsburg Synod (1871) (*Central Conference of American Rabbis Yearbook*, Vol. 1, p. 114), the Pittsburgh Platform of 1885, the Columbus Platform of 1937, and the Centenary Statement of 1976. The Columbus Platform stated: "Revelation is a continuous process, confined to no one group and to no one age. Yet the people of Israel, through its prophets and sages, achieved unique insight in the realm of religious truth. The Torah, both written and oral, enshrines Israel's ever-growing consciousness of God and of the moral law. It preserves the historical precedents, sanctions and norms of Jewish life, and seeks to mould it in the patterns of goodness and of holiness." The Centenary Perspective (1977) stated: "Torah results from the relationship between God and the Jewish people. The records of our earliest confrontations are uniquely important to us. Lawgivers and prophets, historians and poets gave us a heritage whose study is a religious imperative and whose practice is our chief means to holiness. Rabbis and teachers, philosophers and mystics, gifted Jews in every age amplified the Torah tradition. For millennia, the creation of Torah has not ceased and Jewish creativity in our time is adding to the chain of tradition." Each of these documents and others have stressed that we adapt basic ideas and specific practices to our own needs based upon the underlying biblical and rabbinic thought. The process of adaptation relies on the tradition, precedent, *minhag*, and the mood of the age. We have always been governed by a strong feeling for historical process which has led to radical change, although that fact has not been acknowledged by Orthodox authorities. During the early years of the Reform movement, it was not clear how far-reaching such changes might be; there were radicals who saw no limits, and they have continued to have disciples to this day. The vast majority of Reform Jews have made their changes within a broad framework whose outlines have become fairly clear, as shown by the debates of the annual rabbinic conferences and the decisions of the Responsa Committee. We have added to these outlines through *Shaarei Mitzvah*, the *Shabbat Manual*, and other similar works.

A third element leading toward some degree of authority within the Reform movement is the Responsa Committee, which was created in 1906. Although no responsa appeared until 1911, they have been issued ever since both by the Conference and by various individuals within the Conference, particularly Solomon B. Freehof. In introductions to various volumes of responsa, Solomon Freehof has made it quite clear that the responsa are to be considered as guidance, not governance, but actually, in view of the lack of enforcing power within the Orthodox community, this is equally true for modern Orthodoxy. The large number of questions directed to the Responsa Committee annually— e.g., during the last year more than sixty such questions have come to the committee or its chairman—clearly indicate that some Reform Jews seek a measure of authority and guidance from the past for their current actions. As Samuel Cohon stated: "Reform Judaism relied upon tradition, progressive revelation, and reason for its decision while the very nature of Reform Judaism led to somewhat diffuse authority" (Samuel S. Cohon, "Authority in Judaism," *Hebrew Union College Annual*, Vol. XI, pp. 593ff.).

The authority of Reform *halacha*, therefore, lies in divine revelation, the tradition both written and oral, as interpreted by scholars of the past and our own time for our day. As there is no enforcing mechanism for any decisions which may come from such interpretation except the will of the people, all such decisions seek to provide guidance to the individual, and we hope that they will be followed. We may, therefore, see that diversity, individualism, and tradition have played equally decisive roles in traditional Judaism and Reform Judaism. It is not that the sources of authority differ particularly, but the willingness to use various sources as a way of guiding Judaism and influencing the Jewish people is very distinctive. Orthodox Judaism has felt threatened and endangered for several generations. Therefore, it has been unwilling to make the kind of radical changes necessary for the times. It has overlooked the willingness and ability of the Tannaim, the Amoraim, the Geonim, the Rishonim, and the Aharonim to make changes. They always changed the outer forms in keeping with the inner spirit and adapted Judaism to radically different situations. Reform Judaism has followed this path, while traditional Judaism has lost its nerve. The diversity which we, therefore, continue to permit is part of the general pattern of Jewish life. It has and will add to the richness of our heritage and, of course, has affected and will affect all Jews throughout the world.

RABBINIC AUTHORITY: THE HUMAN ELEMENT

Joseph Rudavsky

We have gathered here to take a hard look at ourselves, our roles, our strengths and our weaknesses. We do so from the perspective of the authority we bear as rabbis in Israel. We are searching and questioning. Our search is flawed by the reality factor that we live in a world of illusion and delusion circumscribed by such determinants and limitations as what we are and what we would like to be. In this process we can isolate three elements.

How do we perceive ourselves, our roles, our authority, our prerogatives? How would we like others to perceive us—our roles, our authority, our prerogatives? How are we actually perceived? It is unclear to us who we are and what we are. This program is evidence of the fact. It covers twenty approaches to rabbinic authority given as Torah sessions in a Pittsburgh hotel followed by a presentation in the sanctuary of Rodef Shalom entitled "Today's Rabbinate: The Personal Equation." It too will consist of nineteen individual discussions. We may thus conclude that from Pittsburgh Torah will come forth, while from the sanctuary, personalism will blossom.

In addition, to illustrate our confusion in preparing for this subject, the discussion leaders were provided with a bibliography listing 150 articles of interest on the rabbinate. To each we may apply the talmudic word: *Alu v'alu divrey Elohim hayim*. What initially should concern us is the definition of the terms we are using, particularly the terms "rabbi" and "authority." There are two different views of the term "rabbi" that I should like to focus on. One was offered by Rabbi Morton M. Berman on October 8, 1941, marking the twentieth year of the Jewish Institute of Religion:

> Unlike workers in other trained fields the rabbi has unfortunately no clear, defined sphere of activities upon which to base his authority. What seem to be his special functions can no longer be claimed as his special prerogatives. The rabbi has become an educator among educators, a social worker among social workers, a political reformer among political reformers, an organizer among organizers. The authority which he may claim in these fields he must share with the more expert. In those functions where he seems to be exercising an old prerogative of his own as, for example, in preaching, he is too often merely the echo of these professionals. Even the priestly function, as when he marries and buries, finds him in competition with the state. Thus, lacking a special function, he has no authority of a special character that gives him warrant to speak to and for the Jews.

The other view was expressed by Max Routtenberg, who held that:

> The American rabbi is a unique phenomenon in Jewish history. There has never been any one quite like him. It is fruitless either to compare or contrast him with any of our past models. He is neither priest nor prophet, neither scholar nor judge, neither "Rav" nor "Rebbe." But he has something of all of them; he is, in

37

effect, a synthesis of all types of creative Jewish leadership of the past. He is unique in another sense, in that he has fused into his pattern of leadership the multiplicity of religious trends and modes of the Jewish past. Except for rare exceptions, he is not an Ashkenazi or a Sephardi, he is not a mitnaged or a hasid, he is not an East European yeshiva bochur or a West European seminarian. He is all of them. He has been influenced by all of them and has absorbed their flavors and nuances, their traditions and customs, blending them with the colors and patterns of his American environment . . .

The second term that we deal with is "authority"—its meaning, as defined by the *American College Dictionary,* is as follows:

Authority, control, influence denotes a power or right to direct the actions or thoughts of others. Authority is a power or right, usually because of rank or office, to issue commands and to punish for violations. Control is either authority or influence applied to the complete and the successful direction or manipulation of persons. Influence is a personal or unofficial power derived from deference of others to one's character, ability or station; it may be exerted unconsciously or may operate through persuasion.

Which of these definitions fits the rabbi? I am partial to the third. To me the critical factor is the human element caught in the biblical "*V'ahavta,* love thy neighbor as thyself." Love includes both you and your neighbor. It deals with relationship, dialogue, and encounter with the self and with other human beings. Only through a proper image of the self can one reach out to others. What must the rabbinic self-image be? We may list several elements. The rabbi must not succumb to the hazards of intellectual arrogance. He serves as a vessel, a *Klee Kadesh,* to transmit a tradition, not to manipulate people. The rabbinic tasks are to be fulfilled with humility.

It is a measure of the limitation of all systems of formal ethics that this, the most fundamental and far-reaching of all human virtues, cannot be commanded. There is no positive precept, "Be humble." Humility is not self-effacement, as the Torah indicates when Moses' humility is praised on the occasion of his uncompromising rejection of the slanders of Miriam and Aaron. Humility means a balanced perspective on life, a proper understanding of one's own place and that of all others in the scheme of things. Humility in a rabbi means a recognition that he is less important than the religious and ethical tradition he is called upon to expound and propagate; that the synagogue is only a means to an end that is greater than itself, designed to help bring the presence of God and His Law into the lives of men. There is more than alliteration linking humility, humor, and humaneness together, for they are all facets of a true sense of values, a capacity to avoid the pitfalls of pride in oneself and depreciation of one's fellow-man.

As rabbis we should be aware of both our capabilities and our limitations and accept them humbly. Put another way, we may appreciate the implications of this as we share a letter which appeared in *American Judaism* in 1959, written by a mother to her son aspiring to be a rabbi. What she wrote then is still true today.

One of your hardest tasks will be to retain your humility. Rabbis receive so much adulation that they have to work to hold on to a sense of perspective and keep themselves from believing all the nice things they hear about themselves. When you speak to your congregation you will be "above" them physically, but it is better to think of yourself as a servant of your flock than as a "commander."

Remember how your own rabbi begins each Yom Kippur service with a plea for humility. Take that prayer seriously.

The rabbi then, as he meets his people, must not meet them with a holier-than-thou attitude, but rather in his own life he should practice the kind of Judaism he preaches, in the light of *Na-eh doresh na-eh m'kayem.*

The personal influence of the rabbi upon his congregants should be the stronger today. The life of the rabbi led in piety is the most convincing instruction for those whom he serves. Leo Baeck has offered what seems to me the most meaningful appraisal of the rabbi's message at its highest: "The message," said Dr. Baeck in an article first published in the *Jewish Guardian,* "the message is not the sermon of a preacher but the man himself. The man must be the message. The rabbi must not deliver a message, he must deliver himself, in terms of convictions that he practices, not only preaches."

Not only must the rabbi consider his own selfhood, but he must be concerned about how he reaches out to encounter others. The key for the rabbi in interpersonal relationships is the word "mensch."

A young student once came for *semichah* to an older rabbi. The young man came through the examination on the four parts of the *Shulhan Aruch* with flying colors, but the rabbi hesitated to give him the coveted document. "What is wrong, rabbi?" the young man asked. "You do not seem to be familiar with the fifth *Shulhan Aruch.*" "I thought there were only four." "Oh, no, there are six. The fifth is *le'olam yehey adam,* how to be a mensch, and the sixth, how to get along with unmenschen!"

We may take the word, then, of Rabbi Joshua as our guide. "*Aseh lecha rav u'kneh lecha chaver. . .* provide yourself a rabbi, thereby get yourself a friend." Note the *vav* in the Hebrew, which implies a double responsibility. As one of the colleagues so beautifully put it—"A rabbi is a shepherd":

> As a shepherd, a rabbi follows in a great tradition. The *Tanchuma* tells us that the Holy One tests the righteous in the pasture. There, David, Amos, and Moses proved themselves.
>
> Like Moshe Rabbenu, therefore, the rabbi is a shepherd. His life is with people. He does not stand on some high hill and point the way. He does not sit in some tall tower and commune only with God. He does not lock the door of his study and bury himself in books. He is a shepherd and his life is with people. He shares their every circumstance. Whether in straight paths or death-darkened valleys, his life is with his people. . . .
>
> The flock cannot know their shepherd nor the shepherd his flock in a few moments or even a few months. The rabbi's truest function is revealed in terms of years, decades, as he watches children grow, marries them, and teaches their children in turn; as he stands beside loved ones around the death bed of some patriarch whom he has come to admire and respect. He most truly is the shepherd when he loves the truant and the wayward, when he can sit and listen to vengefully cruel words of a couple whose marriage is cracking and try patiently and repeatedly to help them.
>
> He is most truly the shepherd when all the members of his flock are precious

to him, personalities to be respected, lives to be touched, souls to guard and to guide through the beauty and the terror of every life's cycle.

Where then does the rabbinic authority lie? It lies in human relationships, in concern, empathy, sensitivity to the needs of human beings. Authority comes from humanity, "menschlichkeit," this is the seed bed for all we preach and teach. This is the second factor of our equation. Another way to express "menschlichkeit" is to acknowledge the reality of the duality of the Jewish obligation—between man and God, between man and fellowman.

The ability to relate to one's fellowman, to share in his joys and sorrows, his moods of exaltation and despair, is fundamental in any kind of rabbinic authority. A modern commentator affirms this when he points out that unlike the usual Jewish prayers, which are almost always couched in the plural, the priestly benediction appears entirely in the singular. Thus, "May the Lord bless you and keep you" is a prayer for the welfare of the individual, and the Midrash comments that the priests were to confer this blessing on a face-to-face basis.

How necessary this is for our times, too! For we must recognize that to this generation the rabbi achieves his authority by his presence. His handclasp to the sick and bereaved symbolizes Judaism's message of comfort and courage. His reassuring counsel in the midst of a family in crisis becomes Judaism's expression of hope for clearer understanding and reconciliation. The rabbi's smile, his word of good cheer at some moment of happiness reflects our religion's spirit of rejoicing and thanksgiving. How much Judaism loses, how meaningless become the very words of Torah that the rabbi speaks, how empty even his prayers, if the people are bereft of his personal blessings in their daily lives.

Colleagues, our authority is vested in our ability to influence, to mold, to direct. It is not automatic, not vested upon us with *semichah*, but through *semichah* we are vested with the challenge and opportunity to earn authority by what we are and what we do. *Semichah* provides the means to build and to plant in the light of the ethics of our fathers, who taught: "The day is short, the task great—we are not called to complete it or to evade it. *Hayom katzar v'hamlacha m'rubah v'lo atta ben chorin l'hibatel mimenah.*"

THE AUTHORITY OF THE TRADITION FOR THE REFORM RABBI

MICHAEL S. STROH

It is, perhaps, significant that the question of rabbinic authority should be raised at this moment in history. That a movement for which the question of *meaningfulness* always took the top rung on the list of priorities should now introduce the question of authority may indicate a shift in perspective. The authority of the rabbinate flows from the nature of the religious role that the rabbi plays. His authority cannot be charismatic, rooted either in a direct call from God or in his own personality, nor can it be priestly, based upon ceremonies which only he can perform for them to be efficacious. Certainly the authority of a Reform rabbi cannot be juridical, anchored in a court which gives him legal authority and provides sanctions for enforcement. The authority of a liberal rabbi is based upon his knowledge of tradition, as it really is, today, for any rabbi. Therefore, the authority of the rabbi is equal to the authority of tradition itself. No authority can flow to the rabbi from a tradition without authority. So the central question we must raise is: what is the authority of the tradition for Liberal Judaism?

The modern world is inhospitable to the authority of a tradition, and historical science has made a sustained attack on it since the nineteenth century. As Jürgen Moltmann puts it, the purpose of historical science is to destroy history.[1] It reveals tradition to be conditioned by contexts; it exposes the causes that underlie beliefs and prescriptions, and, therefore, it liberates us from traditional authority. This process was essential to the birth of Reform Judaism. Now what can it mean for us to turn to the tradition looking for authority?

The modern world is equally inhospitable to religion as the experience of the transcendent. Our time has been described as a time of the absence of God, the death of God, the silence of God. What is absent is the felt power of God, the felt power of God's authority. The experience of the "holy" is almost non-existent in modern culture. This phenomenon is called *secularity*. And to deal with religion at this moment of history, we must understand the origins of secularity, and what "secularity" really means.

Before modern times, which begin in the seventeenth century, the authority for truth lay outside the individual, usually in some tradition. Belief about the nature of ultimate reality and acceptance of an ethical and ritual system were not based upon an inner assent to truth, but on a tradition because of the authority of Him who revealed it, namely God. This is called *heteronomy*. Judaism was characterized by a desire for total heteronomy, bringing the totality of a person's life, his every action, under the authority of God's Law.[2] Modern culture, however, is characterized by *autonomy*, which places authority inside the individual. The individual must respond by an inner assent to the truth of a

41

proposition; an external authority as warrant for truth is simply not enough. This appears in Reform Judiasm as the freedom of the individual to believe and observe what is personally meaningful to him.

In order to understand the present situation and its problems we must examine how European civilization moved from heteronomy to autonomy. We will examine three historical phenomena which have led to the present secular climate: the development of technology, the rise of capitalism, and the history of Western philosophy itself. Let us begin with technology. The first fruit of technology is the development of modern communications, leading not only to increased knowledge about the world but to the placing of all systems of thought and feeling next door, so to speak, so that nothing appears that alien. The result is what the sociologist Peter Berger calls a system of multiple plausibilty structures. Once many structures seem plausible, doubt is cast on the truth and absoluteness of one's own structure. "Thus the institutional pluralization that marks modernity affects not only human actions but also human consciousness: Modern man finds himself confronted not only by multiple options of possible courses of action but also by multiple options of possible ways of thinking about the world. In the fully modernized situation (of which contemporary America may be taken as the paradigm thus far) this means that the individual may choose his *Weltanschauung* very much as he chooses most other aspects of his private existence. In other words, there comes to be a smooth continuity between consumer choices in different areas of life—a preference for this brand of automobile as against another, for this sexual life-style as against another, and finally a decision to settle for a particular 'religious preference.' . . . suffice it to say that there is a direct and sociologically analyzable link between the institutional and the cognitive transformations brought on by modernity. This link can be put in more precise terms: Modernity pluralizes both institutions and plausibility structures . . ."[3] The outcome of doubt about one's own metaphysical system in the face of the plausibility of all others leads to relativism, and possibly the abandonment of all metaphysical systems. The *reductio ad absurdum* of this position is total doubt about ethical systems, political systems, scientific systems, in other words, complete solipsism.

In the realm of faith the naturalness of tradition disappears, and even the person born and raised in a religion has now become "compelled to choose." However, the plausibility of all systems has removed any grounds for choice, and what is required is a "leap of faith." This Kierkegaardian leap in the absence of the feeling of inner certitude about one's inherited doctrinal system is a product of modern perceptions of multi-plausibility and is in the context of the collapse of the assumed authority of one's own tradition. We have not used the scientific method against our own sacred texts and history without paying a price.

Technology itself is more than the neutral use of tools; it is the will to human domination of reality. The world is transformed into natural resources for technological exploitation. We now see the world from this perspective, and even nature is almost never in the raw, but is organized into national parks and conservation areas designed by human beings for human purposes. In the natural world, therefore, *everywhere we look we see only ourselves.*

Capitalism is closely related to technology, and the development of the former parallels the development of the latter. However, capitalism makes its own contribution to the development of modern consciousness. As compared to the Middle Ages, which exalted the virtue of loyalty, both to one's own tradition and to those higher in station, the new *Weltanschauung* exalted the individual, especially the self-determining "rugged individual." Loyalty to the past was replaced by innovation as a primary virtue. The uncritical acceptance of anything was frowned upon, and all were equal in the struggle for survival or truth.

In capitalism the efficient use of matter became the only real value, leading to the philosophical view that only matter is real. When it comes to the bottom line, a medieval person might sacrifice efficiency to nobility, but a capitalist who held any other value than the efficient use of matter would not survive for very long. Capitalism, by self-definition, is an economic system based upon self-interest and it, therefore, produced a human self-understanding based upon self-concern. Its essence can be found in the title of a book by Ayn Rand, *The Virtue of Selfishness*. Early capitalism resulted in the irrelevance of all tradition; it created a person who depended only on his own resources, made his own decisions (autonomy), thought only in terms of himself, saw reality as a projection of himself, understood all value as what met his needs. Such a person can hear only his own voice.

For an analysis of the role that the history of Western philosophy has played in the creation of secular humanity we turn to Martin Heidegger in his book *Nietzsche*. Heidegger, explicating Nietzsche, traces the roots of the problem to Plato's myth of the cave. A group of people are chained in a cave with the light behind them, and all of reality is presented to them as shadows on the cave wall. One of their number escapes to the sunlight, and seeing the real world for the first time, returns to the cave to persuade his fellows that what they take to be reality is only a shadow of reality, an illusion. In this myth we are presented with two worlds, the world of shadows and the world of light. The world of shadows is the material world in which we live; the world of light is the pure ideas, the world of spirit. The illusory world is the material world, the real world, the world of ideas. Thus matter is ultimately unreal; spirit is ultimately real. The modern world has simply turned Plato on his head. The real world is the world of matter; spirit is an illusion. However, the modern world has not overcome Platonism. It still has a two-world theory, but has erased one of the worlds. In the light of this we must ask whether the marriage of Judaism, Christianity, and Islam to Greek philosophy has proven beneficial or not, whether Athens has vanquished Jerusalem to the misfortune of Jerusalem and Judaism.

To Nietzsche the phrase "God is dead" meant the death of the super-sensible world, the world of spirit. How we journeyed from Plato to the modern consciousness was described by Nietzsche as follows:

1. The true world, attainable for the wise, the pious, the virtuous man—he lives in it, he is it.
2. The true world, unattainable for now, but promised for the wise, the pious, the virtuous man ("for the sinner who repents").

3. The true world, unattainable, indemonstrable, unpromisable, but even as thought, a consolation, an obligation, an imperative.
4. The true world, unattainable? In any case, unattained. And as unattained also unknown. Consequently, also, not consolatory, redemptive, obligating: to what could something unknown obligate us?
5. The "true world"—an idea which is of use for nothing, which is no longer even obligating—an idea become useless, superfluous, consequently, a refuted idea: let us abolish it!
6. The true world we abolished: which world was left? the apparent one perhaps? . . . but no! along with the true world we have also abolished the apparent one![4]

This means the disappearance of God, values, and transcendent meanings; in other words, the coming of nihilism. We are left only with ourselves and the earth. The world of the spirit, then, becomes unreal material projection. So to Feuerbach God is a projection of ideal humanity, to Freud a projection of the father, to Marx God and the entire world of spirit are a reflection of the material substructure. For Sartre existence in such a universe (the only real one) is absurd and devoid of meaning. And so it is.

Our modern world, then, has created a new human being: seeing reality as a potential for technological re-creation in his own image, appropriating reality as if it existed to meet his needs, believing that only matter is real, unable to find a secure framework for belief and action, traditionless, living nihilistically without values that can compel behavior. Perhaps this new human being found his expression in the Nazi film *Triumph of the Will* made by Leni Reifenstahl. Such a person can contemplate technologically organized mass murder.

Thus, the ideas that liberated Western humanity from the burdens of tradition and that made possible the creation of democracy, and the belief that all individuals, including Jews, are equal under the law, and must have equality of opportunity as a natural right, when taken to their ultimate consequences may prove ultimately destructive. It may be that the reappropriation of tradition will bring salvation not only to Jews but to humanity. How is it possible to do this?

We must reject the possibility that we will renounce autonomy and return to the tradition, medievally understood. We must renounce it for two reasons. History does not move backward, and there is no possibility of re-creating a pre-technological era. Any Orthodox Jew with a television is aware of many plausible structures and must consciously choose to be Orthodox. The naturalness of tradition is over for him too. Secondly, it is not all bad. We would not want to give up democracy or the right to use our critical intelligence rather than accept all arguments based on authority. Our path must be forward, and not backward.

The question is whether any partial acceptance of Enlightenment ideas is possible or only their total acceptance or total rejection. I believe that partial acceptance is possible. We must reject the two-world theory of matter and spirit that flows from Plato and is not found in the Jewish tradition before the circumcising of Greek philosophy. We must reject the Kantian version of autonomy in which the human person is self-legislating and, therefore, self-sufficient. If there is any hope for a return to the transcendent in a Jewish sense, then God legislates and we listen. The tradition contains authority within it, but is not an absolute and infallible source of authority. In Gershom Scholem's terms we are religious anarchists in that we do not accept a unitary authority. However, the tradition is the only source of authority we have; it is the only witness to God's authority that we have as Jews. There must still be individual judgment and decision in interaction with the tradition as a source of nonunitary authority. Our decisions are not infallible.

We possess two approaches. We can bring to bear on the tradition our critical intelligence and all the tools of reasoning and scientific investigation we have developed until now as methods to understand the tradition as a source of authority. Hopefully we can learn to use these tools for constructive and not destructive purposes. This approach was pioneered by the classical Reformers, such as Abraham Geiger. While we may not share all their philosophical premises or agree with all their conclusions, we would not want to dispense with critical intelligence altogether. What do we share with Geiger? The belief that substantial change has taken place in history, and that human reason can comprehend some of the processes involved in that change. Reform has rejected the idea that time passes but nothing really changes. While the study of history can have destructive consequences for traditional authority, it was Geiger's point of view that a study of Jewish history would enable us to understand how that authority has manifested itself in the midst of historical change, and thus provide valuable insights into our own period, and ways of ensuring the creative continuity of Jewish tradition. Historical study reveals the uniqueness of the Jewish experience. Toynbee could not fit the Jewish people into patterns which held for all other civilizations, so he considered them a fossil. We, however, in the spirit of Krochmal, can interpret the facts differently and see transcendent purpose to the uniqueness of Jewish existence.

Since the discussion of mitzvot has never been a nonrational process in Judaism, the use of reason to analyze the nature of continuity and change should be a viable method for a better understanding of the Jewish tradition and its authority. It is a use of intelligence to help solve our problems. Without the concept of substantial change in history, there is no basis for treating Judaism as a dynamic rather than a static system. If Judaism is not inherently, by its nature, a dynamic system, then Reform Judaism is not legitimate. The nature of the development of the Jewish tradition is discovered by historical study. It is also possible that we can obtain insights into the dynamism itself, and use these insights productively.

Secondly, we can use the approach of Franz Rosenzweig, who is very helpful in our present discussion. His premises, namely, that the tradition is authoritative, that it is authoritative in its entirety and not only in what can be comprehended rationally, that in the modern age individuals must interact with the tradition and make personal decisions about what they can affirm and incorporate into their lives—all are the premises we would have to accept to affirm both the authority of tradition and the realities of modern consciousness.

Reformers like Geiger looked at the Jewish tradition with a Hegelian bias. We no longer believe in continuous progress, nor that the later is always more true than the earlier. The belief that only universal ethics are mitzvot and "with ceremonies one does not stand on ceremony" is not a belief that we share. We are fully committed to the significance of the particularities of Jewish existence. Rosenzweig is well suited to speak to our postmodern sensibilities. With him we are dealing with a God who commands, not a "God-idea." To Rosenzweig the entire tradition was authoritative, its ethical and ritual components, its universal and particular aspects. He recognized, however, that our autonomous situation is substantially different from the heteronomous situation of the past. It is the individual who must respond *"na'aseh v'nishma"* for the mitzvah to be a reality, yet he responds to mitzvot issuing from an authoritative tradition. Rosenzweig believed that not everything can be comprehended rationally, neither in the realm of Jewish history nor in the realm of mitzvot. "Meaningfulness" is to respond to a commandment, and meaningfulness is not always rational. Rosenzweig never would say that any particular mitzvah was meaningless; his response was that he did "not yet" observe it. The future is open. Since the Reform movement now finds meaningful mitzvot that once were relegated permanently to the museum, we should understand his plea to keep the future open. Somewhere between the idealists' method for deciding with precision between the kernel and husk in the Jewish tradition and the existentialists' lack of method, we must find our place.

If our search for authority in the Jewish tradition is to be rewarded with success, we must begin with the presupposition that the tradition does have authority over us, and our task is to discover that authority. If we cannot presume that, or if our search reaches a dead end, then I am afraid that neither the tradition nor the rabbinate possesses authority in any meaningful sense, and if any other authority can be discovered it will supersede Judaism and render the rabbinate a meaningless institution. If no source of authority whatever can be found, then we are doomed to nihilism, and a world we would not want to live in.

NOTES

1. Moltmann, Jürgen, *Theology of Hope*, London: SCM Press Ltd., 1965, pp. 236–237.
2. Ricoeur, Paul, *The Symbolism of Evil*, Boston: Beacon Press, 1967, pp. 118–139.
3. Berger, Peter, *The Heretical Imperative*, Garden City: Anchor Press/Doubleday, 1979, p. 17.
4. Heidegger, Martin, *Nietzche*, Vol. 1, *The Will to Power as Art*, San Francisco: Harper and Row, Publishers, 1961, pp. 203 ff. Cf. also Nietzsche, Friedrich, *The Twilight of the Idols*, New York: 1968, pp. 40–41.

RABBI, AN INTERPRETER OF RELIGIOUS EXPERIENCE

PETER S. KNOBEL

Rabbi Harold Saperstein in his Convention address, "The Authority of the Rabbi," states:

> Rabbis can claim authority on the basis of scholarly qualifications. This no longer implies mastery of *halacha* which carries no compulsion for the liberal Jew.[1] Nor does it imply, as it did several generations ago, ability to transmit general culture. Many of our congregants are our equals or superiors in this regard. Nor is it measured by the ability to discuss timely issues. Here we face competition or public media professionals. Torah for the modern Jew must be the total spectrum of Jewish values. It is from this context that the rabbi must be able to deal with problems of life and society. The rabbi is the expert in Judaism.[2]

The métier of the rabbi is Judaism. The rabbi is the Judaic expert. These statements are unexceptionable. The focus of this paper is to state explicitly the nature of the scholarly qualifications and expertise of the rabbi and thereby to propose a curriculum for rabbinic study and rabbinic education.[3]

The well-known and often quoted Mishnah from the beginning of Avot is the *locus classicus* of rabbinic claim to authority:

> Moses received Torah[4] at Sinai and transmitted it to Joshua, and Joshua to the elders, and the elders to the prophets, and the prophets transmitted it to the members of the Great Synagogue.

The chain of rabbinic transmission is subscribed to either literally, as is the case with Orthodox rabbis, or at least symbolically, as is the case with most Reform and Conservative rabbis. The rabbinate and its function, as well as its authority, are linked to the Sinaitic experience and to Moses as the archetypical rabbi. As Jacob Neusner has pointed out:

> What unites all historical forms of the rabbinate is devotion to "study of Torah" by which was meant both Scriptures as we have them and the Oral Revelation handed on by God to Moses.[5]

The historical expectation and the expectation of the average Jew is that the rabbi is an expert in Torah. (In Orthodoxy this has tended to mean that he is a halachic expert, and in Reform it has tended to mean an expert in Jewish values.)[6] The rabbi is the transmitter, exegete, and exemplar of Torah.[7] This is the rabbi's unique role and his/her only authentic source of authority.[8] No matter what other skills the rabbi possesses, to lead and to serve the Jewish people the prime source of that leadership and service must be Torah. That the rabbi is a teacher of Torah is neither novel nor particularly illuminating unless one gives a much more precise definition of Torah and what it means to teach Torah.

47

Torah is the full corpus of books which have been included in the canon in Judaism. It includes both the written and oral Torah and not merely Tanach with a few aggadic citations. Torah is an open-ended canon. Contemporary theology lacks a comprehensive assessment of Judaism drawn from the full canon. Gershom Scholem describes the three creative stages in Judaism as biblical, rabbinical tradition, and kabbalah:

> What the three stages have in common is their unapologetic character, as is particularly evident in aggadah and kabbalah. The thought process of the latter tend to be communicated unreflectively and they forge their own justification as against other categories. In this they differ essentially from theological literature to medieval philosophy of religion . . . as well as from the more modern reflections on Judaism. . . . The outstanding characteristic of these theologies, regardless of their basic difference, is their strictly selective attitude toward tradition. They disregard anything they find indigestible and by its nature unsuitable for apologetic purposes.[9]

A similar observation is made by Jacob Neusner:

> When you read the work of nearly all modern contemporary voices of Judaism, what books must you know to understand their thought? And what do you need *not* to know? It is commonplace that you must know Kafka and will do well to know Hegel. You should also know some stories and sayings of Hebrew Scriptures, the written Torah and some tales of the Talmud and Midrashim, the oral Torah. . . . In my judgment Judaism cannot draw for definition solely upon written Torah and episodic citations of rabbinic aggadah.[10]

The rabbi must not be merely a master of citation, one who has the homiletic skill to draw the proper pithy saying to meet the immediate situation. The rabbi must be the one who, understanding the process and the modes of thought which created Torah in the past, now creates Torah anew. The rabbi's task is thus essentially theological. It is the translation of experience and deeds into moments of transcendence. Through the rabbi-theologian the process of Torah is continued by opening up the path to religious experience and by raising deeds to the level of mitzvot. By renewing the Torah process through study of the whole corpus, I believe that we can begin to recover a normative stance on Jewish values which will be ideologically compelling and practically implementable. The creative periods of the past have drawn on the full canon. The current efforts need to be similarly directed.

What is the way in which Torah grew? From the available options why were some selected and others rejected? How was historic experience of the Jewish people raised to the level of Torah? What were the inner dynamics of Torah? How can the language of Torah shape Jewish people's understanding of reality? These are some of the questions which must be asked and answered.

There are two trends in contemporary Reform Judaism which appear to me to hold real promise: The reconsideration of the mystical tradition and the reconsideration of halacha. The former is an attempt to recover spirituality or religious experience and to redress an over-evaluation of the role of reason. The latter is an attempt to reestablish discipline and normative values by setting forth ideal patterns of doing that can shape reality in terms of the holy. These trends are not antithetical and they often reside in the same individual simultaneously.

An adequate contemporary theology will need to assess both of these trends and incorporate both of them. The model should be both aggadah and halacha, *Moreh Nevuchim* and *Mishneh Torah*, Kabbalah and *Shulhan Aruch*. A living Judaism must speak to the inner life of humanity and must be world-creating and world-transforming.

Religious experience is captured in myth and in story. Lawrence Kushner writes: "Every religious revival seems to be accompanied by a rebirth of the narrative as a vehicle for religious truth."[11] The personal encounter between the divine and the human cannot be adequately described, but it can be conveyed by a story told by one to whom it occurred. The appeal here is not to reason but to spirit. It is the testimony of religious imagination. What is required is the revival of the creative impulse that permits religious experience to be a legitimate part of liberal religion and not only the possession of evangelicals and hasidim. Events are true because they do not happen only once but are repeated in our lives.[12] "All true theology is personal. God meets one of us and we in turn are compelled to tell a story from which no objective theological truth can be distilled. For this reason, authentic Godtalk must always begin with the introduction *ma'aseh sh'hayah*. 'It once happened. . . .' "[13]

Kushner provides a number of excellent examples. The following I find most striking:

Another One's Tefilin

Tefilin are small black leather boxes containing bits of parchment on which are written prescribed paragraphs from the Torah. With leather straps they are bound. . . . "for a sign upon thy hand and for frontlets between thine eyes". . . . upon the forehead and the arm each morning. It is an act of personal devotion and obedience to the Master. Now these days tefilin are only regularly worn by observant traditional Jews. The rest of us wear them with less frequency in between which times we store these sacred utensils in the back of the drawer where we also keep our socks. I happen to have an idiosyncrasy when it comes to tefilin. Whenever I travel overnight, I carry my tefilin with me. I tell myself that just in case the spirit should move me, or if I should feel spiritually weakened, I would have them with me. Well, what can I say, after maybe several dozen trips I still haven't put them on but a few times. Nevertheless I still carry them. I even suggested once that I had stumbled upon some new commandment. The commandment of carrying your tefilin with you to hotel rooms.

Then the other day a dear friend told me that his mother had given away his set of tefilin. There were tears in his eyes when he told me.

And then I understood why I had carried my "unused" tefilin with me all this time. They weren't mine. I was only bringing them to their intended owner. "They must be yours," I said.[14]

The revival of the narrative is a significant development which can help to restore the personal element and the return of individual relationship with God to a more prominent place. The rabbi needs to tell his or her own story. The story of the rabbi is a religious story which involves encounter with God. To share it means risking privacy, opening oneself to scrutiny and skepticism, but unless the rabbi's own story is part of Torah, there is little opportunity for congregants to see their lives as religious stories. The religious tales of the past become the tales of the present when they are relived in the present.

Creation, Revelation, and Redemption are primary religious concepts which need expression in contemporary Jewish theology. They are part of the mythic scheme which gave a sense of meaning and purpose to Jewish and human existence in the past. "The Creation is admittedly not conceivable in terms of the first chapter of the Book of Genesis, nor Revelation in terms of Exodus 20 or Redemption in terms of Isaiah's imagery—and yet all these contain a core which would be capable of a new articulation in our time."[15]

We require a new myth, a new sacred story based on the old, which explains the origins of the cosmos and our place in it. The Holocaust and the rebirth of Israel are events which are shaping our collective consciousness. The reemergence of the Lurianic myth in our time is a foretaste of the theological work that needs to be done. Demythologizing was the important task of the eighteenth and nineteenth centuries, but remythologizing of the religious consciousness is the important work of the last quarter of the twentieth century.[16]

Myth and narrative are the aggadic aspects of the rabbi's interpretative task. They are the exegesis of experience in terms of the language of Judaism, the return and experience of the individual and the Jewish people from the realm of the secular to the sacred. They provide emotional and intellectual support for the whole notion of a religious life, but are not sufficient in and of themselves. They do not create a theology of deeds.

"The coming task of theology in Judaism is to define Judaism through the theological study of the now neglected canon of the halacha."[17] Judaism's most dramatic theological expression is in the pattern of deeds (mitzvot) performed by its adherents. The study and interpretation of the halachic corpus will reveal its inner structure and the way it seeks to create a world built on the paradigm of the holy.

> Judaism is a world-creating and world-explaining system. The system, as is obvious, works through law. The law, moreover, functions through processes of argument and discussion. These processes make intelligible and bring under control of rules all of those fresh data of the world which together, at a given point, constitute time and change. The system persists because it makes sense of all data and draws within its framework the newest facts of life. When it can no longer deal credibly with the world within its vast, harmonious framework of rational inquiry and reasonable dispute, of exegesis of the canon in the light of the newest concerns of the age, and the newest concerns of the age in the light of the canon, the system collapses.[18]

The collapse of the halacha in the modern period is a fact of life for most Jews. However, there is a strong sense among many of the need for discipline and the recovery of a normative stance. The Reform movement has recognized this by the production of the *Shabbat Manual, Shaarei Mitzvah,* and the forthcoming *Shaarei Mo-eid.* These are selective and cautious but creative attempts.[19]

Jacob Neusner has proposed a sweeping, creative, and constructive work which lays down statements of continuing norms for a new context and renews the ancient norms through the lessons of a new age.[20]

> We cannot, therefore, concede that the theological work is done for all time in the pages of Maimonides' Mishneh Torah or Shulhan Aruch. We insist that the work is to be done in our own days when decisions are made which bespeak a vision of who we are and what we can be, of what it means to be in God's image and to live in a community meant to express God's will. The ancient, medieval, and modern rabbis did and do more than a work of history and hermeneutics. On the basis of what their eyes are trained to see and their minds to perceive, in each succeeding age they forge a new and contemporary understanding of a new and unprecedented world. That was what was original for them: Maimonides does not merely quote the ancient sources, though Mishneh Torah is a melange of quotations. Through his reflection and arrangement he says something new through something a thousand years old. What we have to learn is that the halachic process contains the theological process of Judaism. When we understand how that process works, we shall gain access to Judaism. The reason is that the halachic corpus contains such vision as we have, and have to share, about the sacred potentialities of humanity and of the human community. The tasks of theology today begin in the exegesis of exegesis done. But they lead to the doing of the exegesis of this time, the interpretation of our world and its days. The creation of worlds goes on in worlds without end. That is what, as Rashi says, it means to be "like God"—to create worlds.[21]

Professor Neusner's own studies of the Mishnah provide a paradigm for the kind of theological work that he is speaking about in the above quotation. In an article which appeared in the *Journal of Reform Judaism*, entitled "Transcendents and Worship through Learning—The Religious World View of the Mishnah,"[22] Professor Neusner summarizes his conclusions. He makes the point that the Mishnah is first of all fundamentally an ahistorical document. It does not appeal to the authority of the past, and it does not represent itself as an exegesis of the Tanach. The Mishnah seeks to set down timeless judgments and set forth principles that are not subject to the scrutiny of historical criticism. The Mishnah prefers to discover the principles of order, in concrete problems of daily life, by substituting the criterion of reason and criticism for that of history and functionality. By means of reason, transcendent considerations are discovered in ordinary things and the acts of daily living. The underlying supposition which governs the Mishnah is that order is better than chaos. By rational discourse and argument, the Mishnah constructs and orders existence, the relationships among people and things are made intelligible. Order and rationality are discoverable because human beings are created in God's image, which means to possess consciousness, mind, and rationality. These make us like God. As Neusner puts it, "the single whole Torah in two forms underlies the one seemingless reality of the world."[23] The search for the unity is hidden by the pluralities of the trivial world. The supposition is that some one thing is revealed by many things.

"These represent in intellectual form the theological and metaphysical conception of a single, unique God, creator of heaven and earth, revealer of one whole Torah, guarantor of unity and ultimate meaning of all human actions and events."[24] Since we are like God in sharing mind, we are able to penetrate God's

intent and plan through the study of Torah. For the rabbis who created the
Mishnah, studying Torah is a mode of obtaining transcendence. "The holy
person," according to Neusner, "is the one who is able to think clearly and
penetrate profoundly into the mysteries of Torah."[25]

The rabbis of the Mishnah were therefore able to create a world which was
comprehensible, a world which made sense, a world in which life had meaning
and purpose. Out of diversity they were able to create unity and order.

It is interesting to note that Professor Blumenthal, in writing about the Zohar,
indicates that the zoharic conception of the relationship between God and
humanity is that we are able to penetrate the mysteries of the Divinity because
we share the quality of having mind. "The Zohar teaches that personal
consciousness is of the essence of God, that personal consciousness is the
common element in man and God—the image of God in which man was
created."[26] Both mysticism and rational halachic study agree on this essential
point. The theological task for the contemporary rabbi is the restoration of the
unity of these two principles: religious experience and ordered life. By laying
bare the inner workings of the halachic process and by addressing anew the
questions of who we are and what we can become, we will begin the creation of
new halacha,[27] a new normative stance—a normative stance which is made up of
deeds. The only true testimony of what we believe comes from what we do. A
theology of deeds will be a restoration of the authentic Jewish way of life—a life
of mitzvot.

The recovery of narrative, of myth, of religious experience and mitzvot is a
theological task. The rabbi is the one who helps to shape the form and substance
of Jewish living. Torah is the story of the Jewish people and its relationship to
God, and the way in which it translates the notion of being created in the image
of God into a life of mitzvot. The source of rabbinic authority, then, is Torah
scholarship, which gives Jewish form and substance to Jewish lives.

NOTES

1. While the statement in general reflects the current situation, it is not wholly true nor
is it a situation which is necessarily to be applauded.

2. See above pp. 24–25.

3. By rabbinic study I mean the personal program of the individual rabbi, and by
rabbinic education I mean the program of study at the College-Institute. The methods of
study and the questions which were addressed to the texts when I was a rabbinic student
do not seem adequate today. The study of Judaism at the College-Institute should draw
heavily on the methods which are being applied to the study of religion in secular
universities. It is the inner dynamic of the text and what it means that are important.

4. Torah here means both *Torah shebiktav* and *Torah shebe-al peh*. It is significant that
the authorities of the Mishnah consider Mishnah to be Torah. This fact has affected the
whole history of Jewish thinking and is an insight which can be applied to the
contemporary.

5. Neusner, *Talmudic Judaism in Sasanian Babylonia* (Leiden: Brill, 1976), p. 46.

6. See the quotation from Rabbi Saperstein above.

7. See the documentation which accompanies Rabbi Saperstein's paper.

8. Personal charisma and congregational acceptance may be important from a practical
standpoint, yet without Torah they lack the necessary substance to sustain Judaism,
although the individual rabbi may enjoy a fruitful career and be beloved based on them.

9. G. Scholem, *On Jews and Judaism in Crisis* (New York: Schocken, 1976), pp. 264-
265.

10. Jacob Neusner, *Method and Meaning in Ancient Judaism* (Missoula: Scholars Press, 1979) p. 191.

11. Lawrence Kushner, *Honey from the Rock* (San Francisco: Harper & Row, 1977), p. 16.

12. Lawrence Kushner, p. 16. Arthur E. Greene, "Jewish Mysticism in a Contemporary Theology of Judaism." *Shefa Quarterly* I, No. 4, September 1978, p. 35.

13. Lawrence Kushner, p.16.

14. *Ibid.*, p. 48.

15. G. Scholem, p. 279.

16. Arthur E. Greene, p. 40.

17. Jacob Neusner, *Method and Meaning in Ancient Judaism*, p. 193.

18. *Ibid.*, pp. 194-195.

19. So far in these halachic areas the subject of ethics has not been addressed.

20. J. Neusner, p. 198.

21. *Ibid.*

22. Spring, 1978, pp. 15-29.

23. *Ibid.*, p. 28.

24. *Ibid.*

25. *Ibid.*

26. David Blumenthal, *Understanding Jewish Mysticism* (New York: Ktav, 1978) p. 113. Also his discussion of Lurianic Kabbalah, p. 177.

27. I have used the word *halacha* in this paper deliberately because it is provocative and because I believe that it indicates the seriousness of the work to be done. This is a call for the creation of something new and not merely a restoration of the old.

THE SUBTLETIES OF OUR RABBINIC AUTHORITY

Samuel E. Karff

Occasionally on the tennis court a ball will waver (for what seems like an eternity) before falling on one or the other side of the net. If the ball drops in my favor it is not uncommon for my opponent to make some quip about "unfair competition" or my "invisible means of support" unless he happens to be a rabbi.

My glib response to such a remark is: "Sorry, wish it were so, but I'm in sales, not administration." Only partly in jest that person was making some allusion to my rabbinic power or authority which, cutely but vigorously, I felt impelled to disavow.

Other strange things happen to rabbis on tennis courts. I had just completed two sets and my opponent, a member of my congregation whom I rarely see at temple, thanked me for the game and proceeded to ask how Larry was doing. Larry is a sweet man, known to both of us, a man in his late sixties who has had an abundance of *tsurus*. His wife died two years ago after intermittent illness. His son died while serving his country. His daughter, in her early forties, died suddenly last year. At the time of this conversation on the court, Larry was recovering from a stroke which impaired his speech.

My tennis adversary remarked: "It's so unfair, such a great guy. He's done so much good and look at all he's had to suffer; and guys like me, who've done so little, lead charmed lives."

Almost without pause, he continued: "You must hear these things all the time." He proceeded to explain that he was "very religious" when he was young, that his mother found the Hitler era an insurmountable obstacle to faith, and that the family quit the synagogue after his Bar Mitzvah. He spoke wistfully and yearningly as if he were saying: "Can you show me a way and a reason to return?"

How did I respond? Only by suggesting that the questions raised were important and tough. He soon realized that after a draining tennis match I was in no mood for a theological discussion. I did not invite him to join me for beer or Gatorade. I play tennis to get away from theodicy.

I

One thing is certain: this particular conversation was held because I was a rabbi. Presumably, the issue raised was as intrinsic to my calling as a question on the Dow Jones trend would be to a stockbroker. I was being cast as defender of the faith and I probably missed a teachable moment by not pursuing the matter.

Subtly, but unmistakably, I had just been confronted by an important aspect of my rabbinic authority. I had been addressed as a specialist in life's meaning, the special agent of a covenant which affirms that in spite of Larry's experience, life is filled with the presence of God.

So often this dimension of our role is lost in conventional definitions of the rabbinate. In his popular little classic *Basic Judaism*, Steinberg, one of the greatest rabbis America has produced, wrote: "Rabbis are teachers of the tradition. To say of rabbis that they are teachers is to deny that they are priests. Unlike some other religions, Judaism does not assert of its clergy that they possess spiritual powers . . . which are unavailable to the laity. In its eyes no difference exists except in training between the man at the pulpit and those in the pews. . . . any layman who has the knowledge and the spiritual fitness may conduct worship and, if he has something to say and can get a congregation to listen to him, may preach. . . . In the end the rabbi differs from his Jewish fellows only in being more learned than they, more expert in the tradition they all share. He is a rabbi by virtue of education; his ordination is graduation, his title an academic degree" (*Basic Judaism*, Harcourt, Brace & World, New York, 1947, pages 154-155).

I submit that Steinberg's definition does not adequately capture the subtleties of the episode on the tennis court or the meaning of my words at a funeral service or in a counseling session. My tennis opponent did not address me as an academic expert on theodicy. He addressed me as someone who has studied and is by vocation the proclaimer of a tradition which affirms the power and love of God even in the presence of suffering and evil. My authority stems from having personally wrestled as a Jew with the issue of life's meaning and having made a commitment to God based on an understanding of Judaism. In this context, my authority is related to my being a personal witness and defender of the faith.

II

Steinberg's suggestion that mine is essentially an "academic degree" and that I am not a priest fails to do justice not only to my vocational life but to the rabbinic role reflected in talmudic literature.

We read that Rabbi Abbahu (third-century Palestinian amora) suffered the tragic death of an infant son. His students, Rabbi Jonah and Rabbi Jose, came to comfort him. Out of their reverence for him they did not presume to use the occasion for a *d'var Torah*, which would proclaim faith in God's ways by citing and expounding texts.

But Rabbi Abbahu, who had sustained the terrible loss, urged them to honor him with the customary *d'var Torah*. They declined and urged him instead to offer a word for the occasion. Whereupon Rabbi Abbahu said: (paraphrase) If for all its venality and transience the verdict of an earthly court is to be accepted, how much the more shall we not murmur at the decree of the heavenly court (Jerusalem Talmud, Sanhedrin, Chapter 6, Halacha 10).

We read that when Rabbi Hanina bar Hama (third-century Palestinian amora) lost his daughter he did not weep. His wife chided him. "Is it a hen who has departed from your house?" Rabbi Hanina responded: "One cannot bear two griefs. I suffer enough that I am now childless; must I also weep until I become blind?" (Shabbat 151b). Earlier, when Rabbi Hanina's son died, he accepted it as a just act of God and said his son died because he "cut down the fig tree before it was time." (He violated a mitzvah of the Torah and was punished for his sins.) (Baba Kamma 91b, Baba Bathra 26a)

Such stories of rabbis responding to grief—stories which abound in talmudic literature—are significant because (1) the rabbi's faith is being tested by personal experience and (2) the rabbi is called upon to affirm *his* faith under the most trying circumstances of all.

This role of "defender of the faith" took many forms. Sometimes the rabbi was cast in a polemical encounter with a sectarian or Judeo-Christian or a gentile emperor. He may have been challenged by another rabbi or disciple. Elisha b. Abuya forfeited that role when he concluded that there is no divine justice in the world (J. Talmud, Hagigah, Chapter 1, Halacha 1). Rabbi Yannai acknowledged the difficulty of the role when he said: "It is beyond our power to explain the prosperity of the wicked or the suffering of the righteous" (Avot 4:19). The fact remains: the classic rabbi's authority was not confined to judgment of matters of Jewish law but involved as well the proclamation of life's essential meaning in covenantal terms.

III

In Steinberg's very antiseptic, rationalistic definition of rabbinic authority there is also a more serious omission. We return to Rabbi Hanina bar Hama. An epidemic in Sepphoris did not affect those living on Rabbi Hanina's street. People were angry. They said Rabbi Hanina had refused to pray for them and hence they were afflicted while he was spared.

Rabbi Hanina responded by implying that his prayers could be of no avail as long as the members of the community betrayed the covenant. Subsequently, the same issue arose at a time of drought. A fast was called, but prayers brought no rain. Rabbi Hanina was faulted for failing to use his power. He drew a similar conclusion. Presumably under other circumstances his prayers would have carried special weight. In the end he made some comment and the rain fell (Jerusalem Talmud, Taanit, Chapter 3).

Elsewhere Rava said: ". . . in the years of Rav Judah their entire studies were confined to the laws of Nezikin (civil law and torts) while we studied (much more). Yet Rav Judah merely took off his shoe and the rain came while we cry out and are not heard. But it is because the Holy One, Blessed be He, requires the heart . . ." (Sanhedrin 106b).

The implication is that under some circumstances the rabbi has special "praying power." Elsewhere we discover that the rabbis, or at least some among them, had healing powers.

Steinberg ignores this dimension of the classical rabbinate, and we tend to do the same. We may label it a Hasidic aberration rather than part of the mainstream. Steinberg is correct in suggesting that the authority (power) vested in the ancient rabbi was by virtue of his study of the Torah and his fidelity to its terms. Steinberg's position fails to mention, however, that this life of Talmud-Torah yielded not only halachic but priestly authority.

Jacob Neusner writes of the Babylonian rabbinate in the third and fourth centuries: "The rabbi was the authority in theology, including the structure and order of the supernatural world. . . . Moreover the efficacy of his prayers was highlighted by his purity, holiness and other merits which in turn derived from his knowledge of the secrets of Torah and his consequent particular observances. He could bring rain or cause drought. His blessings brought fertility and his curse, death . . ." (*There We Sat Down*, Abingdon Press, Nashville, 1972, page 79).

IV

We have cited two dimensions of authority not included in most conventional descriptions of the classical rabbinate: (1) The rabbi is defender of the faith and proclaimer of life's meaning in Judaic terms (sometimes in the context of a personal struggle); (2) the rabbi is mediator of God's healing power. These two rabbinic roles are brought together in talmudic accounts of Rabbi Johanan (third-century Palestinian amora).

According to talmudic tradition Rabbi Johanan never knew his parents. His father died before he was born and his mother died at childbirth (Kiddushin 31b). Johanan's adult life was also marked by tragedy. All ten of his sons died before him. (We are told that Johanan could not regard the death of a child as punishment for sin.)

Johanan was apparently a very gifted scholar. He is credited with having been the compiler of the Palestinian Talmud, and as a youth he attended Rabbi Judah Hanasi's academy. Johanan was also a man of great physical beauty. "He was accustomed to go and sit at the gates of the bathing place. He said: 'When the daughters of Israel come up from bathing they look at me and they have children as handsome as I am' " (Ber 20a). Elsewhere he said: "I am the only one remaining of the beautiful men of Jerusalem." Apparently he was not only handsome but conceited (B. Baba Metzia 84a, Ber 20a).

Understandably Johanan was preoccupied with the Book of Job and the transience of our earthly sojourn. When Rabbi Johanan finished reading Job, he said: "The end of man is to die and the end of the beast is to be slaughtered and all are doomed to die. Happy is he who is brought up with Torah and who labors within the Torah and who has given pleasure to his Creator and who grows up with a good name and departs the world with a good name" (Ber 17a).

We have the portrait of a rabbi who, in addition to being a great scholar, was a handsome man, schooled in sorrow, and very much aware of the reality of death. In the face of suffering and death he proclaimed that fidelity to the covenant was the key to life's meaning.

Once when Rabbi Johanan was ill, Rabbi Hanina came to visit him. Rabbi Hanina asked the ailing Johanan: "Are your sufferings dear to you?" (Do you accept them as a chastisement of love?) Johanan replied: "Neither they nor their reward." Whereupon Rabbi Hanina took Rabbi Johanan's hand and healed him.

Subsequently, Rabbi Eleazer ben Pedat took ill. Rabbi Johanan visited Rabbi

Eleazer, who was lying in a dark room. Even in that dark setting Rabbi Johanan's beauty was evident to Rabbi Eleazer. Rabbi Johanan saw that Rabbi Eleazer was crying. He asked him: "Why are you crying?" Eleazer replied: "I am crying over your beauty, which will disintegrate in the dust." Johanan replied: "On this account you have reason to weep." And they both wept.

Meanwhile Rabbi Johanan asked Rabbi Eleazer: "Are your sufferings precious to you?" "Not they nor their reward." Then Johanan said: "Give me your hand." Eleazer gave Johanan his hand and was healed (Ber 5b).

With these sources we have moved beyond the traditional (halachic) role of the classic rabbinate. We are confronted by a rabbi whose authority is shaped by his defense of the faith and his personal struggle to proclaim the covenant in a world of suffering and death. Rabbi Johanan's authority is also defined by his capacity to mediate God's healing power. Eleazer extended his hand to Johanan and was healed.

V

Now let us quickly move to our time and our situation. We readily recognize that our judicial authority is not that of our classical forebears, and our Reform temper adds to the problematic of that eroding halachic authority. Nevertheless, there are some among us who seek to reaffirm basic continuities between our role as *posak din* and that of our forebears. I have no quarrel with that effort. However, the issue I would place before us refers not to halachic authority but to our role as proclaimers of the faith (agadic authority) and as special mediators of the healing power of God (priestly authority). For all the discontinuity between us and our rabbinic forebears, I would suggest that these dimensions of the classical rabbinate still persist in the expectations of laymen and that our own ambivalence toward these roles is part of the problematic of the contemporary rabbinate.

Let us briefly outline some modern tales of the rabbinate, with special reference to the one I know best, my own. We return for a moment to the tennis court. That question my opponent raised after the game would not have been addressed to me if I were not a rabbi. At its best the question ("Why do good people have such *tsuris*?") was being asked not as a taunt, but out of yearning. My questioner was at the very least an "atheist with an ache."

What of the persons we visit in the hospital whom the physician has proclaimed "terminal" and who seem at times resigned to their fate? If able to speak, they often will, with a little prodding, talk about accomplishments and values as well as regrets. It is as if they are helping us write a eulogy which, they dare hope, will affirm the enduring meaning and significance of their days on this earth. In that setting, when we hear their story, we are being asked, as agents of a meaning-restoring covenant, to confirm that this person's life is invested with abiding worth.

The role of reaffirming the faith is especially prominent when we conduct a funeral service. Those in attendance want and need to be comforted. They need to know not only that we share their pain, but that we are able to proclaim, even under such circumstances, the meaning of the human adventure.

Under far less anguished circumstances we may confront (as I did some years ago) a study group of questing intellectuals who tease and wrestle with us, but who want us to hold our own and may also, on some level, want us to win the argument. Is this so different a role from the rabbinic encounter with the *min*, or doubting disciple?

In a variety of situations we are called upon to defend the faith because by our choice of vocation it is assumed we have a special relation to the covenant which binds God and the people Israel. So far I have been spared a great personal tragedy, but have not those of our colleagues who have endured great personal *tsurus* been tested and invested with special power to mediate a sense of life's meaning as defenders of the faith?

VI

Do we also get called upon to mediate God's healing power? We must not dismiss this notion too precipitously. We have all known persons who have asked us to pray for them or their loved ones. At such times do we say: "My prayers are no more effective than yours"? Or do we pray? Many people assume that by virtue of our vocation we stand in a special relationship with the God of the covenant—or at least may help them pray more effectively.

I am reminded of visiting a psychiatrist, a macho man, a super-athlete, who was shocked to learn he needed a triple bypass. He indicated how difficult it was for him to lie there so dependent and face major surgery. He was accustomed to being the dispenser of counsel in the family as well as at the office. Now his own vulnerability seemed so terribly exposed.

I asked him if we could pray together. It was a moment of poignant emotion and real prayer for both of us. I would not presume that my prayer helped pull him through, but I enabled him to permit himself the posture of prayer, and I do not discount the power of prayer. Moreover, I doubt that prayer with a member of our lay visiting committee would have had the same meaning for him at that time.

There is a form of healing in which we rabbis participate even more tangibly. Because we are regarded as the special agents of a tradition which believes in judgment and accountability, we have special power to intensify guilt or mediate self-acceptance. Who would deny that the reduction of guilt and the enhancement of self-acceptance is of healing significance?

Some examples: Judith was separated from her husband. During the separation her husband drove into the garage one afternoon and took his life. The day and a half between the death and the funeral was a period of boundless anguish; anger alternated with deep self-hate.

My attitude toward Judith, especially during the interval between the death and the funeral, and the words spoken at that funeral, were undoubtedly important factors in her capacity to resist the urge to self-loathing despite her complicity in the failure of their marriage. In that situation I helped her accept the love of God. My attitude as rabbi also enabled Judith to hold her husband (not herself) accountable for the final act and to regard her husband's suicide with more compassion.

In ministering to Judith as a rabbi, I had at my disposal symbols and associations far more potent than any psychiatrist could have mustered. I was the surrogate of a tradition that takes moral judgment very seriously, yet I was able to invoke that same tradition's concept of God's acceptance of us in the midst of our brokenness and God's insistence that we sanctify life—and not embrace death. As a rabbi, my acceptance of Judith had a much deeper value at that particular moment than her acceptance by a psychiatrist.

Carol's husband was dying of cancer. For many months she nursed him at home. He insisted that there be no other nursing care. After months away from her supervisory nursing job at the hospital, she faced the prospect of losing the job on which she would depend for a livelihood after his death. Carol was resentful of her husband's attitude (and felt guilty for being resentful). After considerable hesitation she decided to go back to work and provide a nurse to care for her husband part-time.

She discussed the decision with me. I acknowledged her right to do so and attempted to place this judgment in the context of Judaism's concern for her dignity as well as her husband's. This reassurance was an immensely important balm to her troubled spirit. A psychiatrist's blessing would not have held the same significance.

Marjorie called to tell me that her mother was critically ill at the local hospital. In the course of the phone conversation she explained that she was an only child, that her mother invested so much in their relationship, and that she could never admire her mother as much or be as close to her as the mother craved. She loved her mother but could not give her the intimacy the mother sought.

Marjorie felt at times like a sinful daughter who did not live up to the fifth commandment and was especially full of self-reproach at this time of her mother's critical illness. What Marjorie needed from me (her rabbi) was reassurance that human relationships do not always yield what we hope for, that we are flawed and must struggle to do the best we can, that we must not feel guilty for spending some time preparing our children for camp rather than spending every waking moment at the hospital, and that even our imperfect, blemished relationships may be cherished by us and are acceptable to God.

An audible sigh of relief, an earnest "thank you," and the comment, "You'll never know how much you have just helped me," ended our conversation.

VII

Surely we are far removed from the cultural and theological matrix of our rabbinic forebears. We would not attribute specific healing power to ourselves or our colleagues by virtue of our special immersion in a life of Torah study and observance. But in more subtle indirect ways, we do mediate and release our congregants' openness to the realm of the sacred. We can help them pray. We can put them in touch with God's affirmation of human dignity and God's forgiving love and, by virtue of our capacity to speak as persons who have "mastered" the faith and are vocationally committed to it, we possess special power to help people open themselves to the healing presence of God.

We may cringe at the suggestion of such a role, not only because of its sublety and defiance of crisp articulation, but because we find the burden this role imposes greater than the *nachus* it bestows, or because we are able to affirm less than we think a rabbi should, or because the mark of "holy man" strikes us as being corny or presumptuous or neo-hasidic.

Be that as it may, a very significant if subtle aspect of our rabbinic authority is contingent upon our readiness to accept the role of rabbinic priest and the sensitivity and skill with which we enact it.

Of late we have been primarily concerned with restoring the continuity between the halachic authority of our classic forebears and our own halachic role as rabbis. But any inquiry into our authority must focus at least as much attention on our continuing role as defender-witness-proclaimer of the faith and, yes, as mediator of God's presence in the lives of our people.

CAN WE SPEAK OF REFORM HALACHA?

W. Gunther Plaut

The traditional authority of the rabbi derived from the authority of halacha as a compelling foundation in Jewish life. If halacha has lost its meaning in the ambit of Reform Judaism, then the authority of the rabbi, if any, must be based somewhere else. If, on the other hand, we can still speak of halacha, then what value can we ascribe to it? Are we using the shell of a word without its core, and if so, are we not merely covering with a semantic sleight of hand that which in reality does not exist?

By way of introducing my own view of the matter, may I direct you to the two publications of the Conference which approach as closely as any Reform publications have done the concept of halacha. I refer to the *Shabbat Manual* and to *Shaarei Mitzvah*. In the operative parts of both books the word halacha is *prominent by its complete absence*. That is no accident. Some years ago, twelve years to be exact, I came to the conclusion that we could not properly and usefully employ the word halacha and that we had to base our commitments elsewhere and on different foundations.

I

Halacha is by its very nature a historical term, and so is the appellation Reform Judaism. Strictly speaking, halacha is the way of the Fathers applied to our time, and without stretching the terms in any way we may also define Reform Judaism in this manner. Indeed, when the Liberal movement was still young, it was the objective of its founders to reform halacha—it was *not* to reform Judaism itself.

The matter bears repeating: Reform Judaism began as a movement to reform halacha. During the first fifty years the Liberals were concerned primarily with the effort to bring such legal reform about. Only in the post-classical or radical phase did the leaders of the movement attempt to reform (or better restore) Judaism per se. From the days of the Pittsburgh Platform on, their interest shifted away from a reform of halacha. In fact, they now rejected it in form if not in principle, and focused their interests on other aspects of the ancestral faith. When they did this they awarded the palm of victory to the Eastern Reformers, led by David Einhorn, and made Isaac M. Wise drink the cup of defeat.

While the victory of Einhorn's radicalism meant the shriveling of halacha in Reform Judaism, it turned out that in the long run this non-halachic Judaism had very little viability as Judaism. It became transmuted into Ethical Culture, flourished as a Jewishly spirited Unitarianism, spread as a broad and pleasant middle-class establishmentarianism, with American/Canadian banners gaily affixed to it—but it had lost its moorings in Jewish history, and no amount of

63

quotations from the Prophets could hold its rapid metamorphosis into the Jewish segment of the new North American religion. All this would have come as an unpleasant surprise to Einhorn and as a shock to Wise, but we can hardly blame them for not having been prophets.

But can we not recover halacha today for ourselves? we might ask. *My answer is no.* A hundred years ago it might have been possible, but at that time we still had a fair consensus on the foundation of halacha as grounded ultimately in the Divine will—at least insofar as its biblical foundation was concerned. We lack this consensus today. For us, halacha has lost its umbilical cord with the tradition which brought it forth, and that biblical tradition itself has, because of our adherence to critical and historic scholarship, lost its moorings in the Divine origin of the covenant. Not for all, to be sure, but for enough in our movement to make it impossible to speak of a consensus in this area.

But can we not ground halacha in history or the alleged will of the Jewish people, as the Conservative movement on the one hand and Reconstructionism on the other have tried to do? The Conservative movement insists on maintaining the term halacha and sees itself as a legitimate heir and developer of its premises. In that sense Conservatives are where we were a hundred years ago, but I fear they are no more successful than we were. If God no longer provides the secure anchor of the trilogy God–Israel–Torah, then neither history nor peoplehood can fill the lacuna. Neither is compelling enough for the average Reform Jew to say "I must."

I, therefore, counsel that we give up a term on which we can no longer build our edifice of progress. How then do we approach our task of bringing a sense of commitment into Reform Jewish lives, a sense of ought? Though I believe halacha is not operative for us, it is my unshakable conviction nonetheless that without some such operative ought we may have many things but not a Judaism worth its name.

II

Reform is a composite of tradition and of freedom. Either one can be the source of commitment. That is to say, we can derive the ought either from our sense of tradition or from our sense of freedom, and it is in this possibility of choice that we find our Jewish continuity on the one hand and our uniqueness on the other.

I want to give credit here to two of our colleagues, to our late departed Frederic Doppelt and to David Polish, who nearly thirty years ago brought out a little book entitled *A Guide for Reform Jews*. It distinguished between *mitzvot, halachot,* and *minhagim*. Mitzvot related to the root experiences of being Jewish—such as circumcision or the observance of Pesach. The halachot were the ways by which these experiences were transmuted into the actual (e.g., the matzah); and minhagim were the customs which fleshed out the structure (unterführer, Haggadah). I have written elsewhere and I would like to repeat here that we might well utilize this basic idea but simplify it somewhat.

We must begin with where we are as Jews. We begin where our people are in our congregations. In other words, we begin with what they do, not with what we teach them or with what they ought to do, but with the actuality of their practice. We begin with minhag, while tradition begins with halacha.

By its nature, minhag will in most instances be a reflection of tradition. It is our lifeline to the past. From what people do we must now lead them to assume the essentials of their practice as a mitzvah. This assumption is voluntary and emphasizes the aspect of freedom in our movement. We start with what we do traditionally, and then make it freely into something that we decide is our must, our ought, our mitzvah. I would like rabbis to lead their congregants to say, "I not only *do* it, *I must do it* as a Jew."

Note, I have spoken of mitzvah. The origin of mitzvah is ably discussed by four of our distinguished colleagues in *Shaarei Mitzvah* and I will not here duplicate their words. But regardless of the foundation upon which you as a rabbi or your congregants will place your lives and develop nonpractice into practice and practice into mitzvah, it is the ultimate goal to multiply mitzvot as touchstones of Jewish identity and self-fulfillment in the realm of our history.

Thus I come back to the task and the authority of the rabbi. *The rabbi's task is to lead people from minhag* (in the broadest sense: what people do) *to mitzvah.* His authority derives from the knowledge which he brings to both of these pillars of our existence. He does not compel but he urges; he does not enforce but he explains; he leads—and hopefully he does this in no small measure by his own example. He urges people to make mitzvah responses. Thus, it is as model and interpreter of tradition that the rabbi may be said to exude authority today. In this respect we are, I believe, fundamentally different from the past and also from our Orthodox colleagues. Each one of us is judged on personal merit. Tradition protects us but slightly. Authority accrues to us by dint of our knowledge, our lives, our leadership. That is not the way it used to be. It may not be enough for all of us, but I think it enough to vouchsafe a future for our people.

Can we use the term Reform halacha? My view is no. But mitzvah is the basis on which we can form, and in fact have formed, a consensus. That is enough, at least for now. And it will have to do for the Reform rabbi.

SEMICHAH AND ITS RELATION TO *ISHUT**

BERNARD M. ZLOTOWITZ

This paper has two purposes: The study of the evolving institution of the rabbinate and its relation to *ishut*, and its authority and the symbol of that authority—*semichah*.

The evolving institution of the rabbinate: The rabbi was he who was given a new charge to interpret the law that Moses had received, and symbolic of that new authority was *semichah;* for he, like Joshua, took on the power that had originally been Moses'. For just as authority had been passed on to Joshua through the laying on of the hands, so is authority to the rabbi passed on by laying on of the hands. As the rabbi had not only interpreted but expanded and changed the law, so in every generation and in our generation too, we who are rabbis have the authority to interpret, expand, and change certain laws. Good examples are the power to regulate the calendar, impose fines, settle financial disputes, release the *bechor* (the male first-born of a clean animal) for profane use by reason of disqualifying blemishes, annul vows, inflict corporal and capital punishment, and to nullify a Torah law by a legal fiction (Hillel's *prozbul* or the *sota*, i.e., Yochanan ben Zakkai's decision to give up the process of *sota* [when women accused of adultery were forced to drink the bitter waters because adultery was so rampant (Sotah 9:9)]).

In its original sense, *semichah* was the transfer through the hand of a particular power or quality, such as putting the sins of the people on one of two goats (Azazel) (Lev. 16:7–10). Moses in putting his hands on Joshua ("Now Joshua son of Nun was filled with the spirit of wisdom because Moses had laid his hands upon him; and the Israelites heeded him, doing as the Lord had commanded Moses" [Deut. 34:9]) filled him with the spirit of wisdom. This was elaborated in Second Temple times into a whole ceremony.

Candidates sat in the first three rows in the Sanhedrin, and when a position became available, each in turn was ordained with the title of "rabbi" conferred upon him either orally, i.e., by declaration, or in writing. The garb for the ceremony was a *tallit* which the rabbinic candidate donned for the occasion. In fact, it was originally created as an article of dress for rabbinical ordination and not as a means to preserve the mitzvah of *tzitzit*. (In time, the leaders of the community began to wear it, and eventually so did all males. In Eastern Europe, however, it was worn only by married men, so that the women in the balcony could easily distinguish the married from the unmarried.)

The rabbis in attendance then praised the candidate; e.g., at the ordination of Rabbi Zera they uttered the following words: "Not rouged, not painted, and not bedecked, but yet full of grace"; and at the *semichah* of Ammi and Assi: "Ordain for us men like these, not foolish, stupid, and uneducated men" (Ket. 17a; Sanh. 14a). Following the ceremony, the newly ordained rabbi delivered a learned discourse to show that he was indeed filled with the spirit of wisdom. (The

67

ordination formula was: יורה יורה ידין ידין יתיר יתיר. May he decide [on religious questions] יורה? He may decide— יורה. May he decide [on monetary questions] ידין? He may decide— ידין. May he permit [on בכורות firstling, i.e., that it may not be offered up as sacrifice] יתיר? He may permit— יתיר.)

The ceremony of *semichah* was symbolic of the transfer of authority from Moses on, and for this Rabbi Akiva died. Controversy over authority centered in the ceremony of the *semichah* itself, as witnessed by the Jacob Ibn Habib controversy and in our own time with the Israeli rabbinate. The Israeli rabbinate has arrogated to itself the authority to perform weddings even though על פי דין there is no need to have a rabbi anyhow. *Semichah* is not required for an officiant (*m'sader kiddusin*) at a marriage ceremony. Any knowledgeable person who knows the laws of divorce and marriage may officiate (עמהם) כל שאינו יודע בטיב גיטין וקידושין לא יהא לו עסק עמהם. "He who doesn't know well the subject of divorce and betrothals should not be involved with them" (Kid. 6a and 13a). Since the average Jew is not immersed in such laws, it devolves upon the rabbi to determine that there are no impediments to the marriage and then proceed to perform the ceremony.

The same principle holds true for naming children, officiating at a Bar/Bat Mitzvah ceremony, at a funeral service, etc. Any qualified Jew may conduct life-cycle ceremonies. One need not be an ordained rabbi. The rabbi became the officiant at such ceremonies by default. The Jewish community relegated to him a "priestly" status.

The authority of the rabbi is to apply the law or change it—as in the case of an *aguna*, where the rabbis allow testimony, contrary to the Torah (על פי שנים או שלשה עדים יקום דבר), of one witness and even of a non-Jew, a woman, a child, etc., regarding the death of a husband, whose testimony would otherwise not be accepted.

If the past could make changes in issues of personal status via the *sota*, the *aguna*, we have, therefore, the same right in new circumstances to make changes. The issue of descent is a good example. Biblically it is patrilineal, as in the case of Joseph and Moses. But then a shift took place in the rabbinic period and it became matrilineal. (Two other instances where it is matrilineal are: (1) Saying a *mi sheberach* [when a prayer for a sick person is to be offered, the mother's name is recited—not the father's]; and (2) if the mother is a daughter of a *kohen* or a *levi* there is no *pidyon haben* for the male child who "opens the womb.")

The new situation is that the boundaries of Jewish life are no longer the Temple or the king. Power now is in the terms of the law system—*halachah*. Thus the formula of יורה יורה ידין ידין יתיר יתיר now fits the new situation of how the Jew relates to God— יורה —and how he relates to his fellow Jew—ידין— even at times going beyond the law by cutting off hands (Sanh. 72a and 73b) or imposing מלקות and pronouncing capital sentences (Sanh. 52b). And so the power is now in the rabbinate and not in the priest— יתיר בכורות. Now who determines how you relate to God and to your fellow Jew becomes a focus of controversy. And this is exemplified by the Palestinians against the Babylonians (ultimately the Babylonians win, which accounts for the Bavli being accepted over against the Yerushalmi).

Just as the examples of the *sota* and the *aguna* are changes in personal status beyond the law or against the law, so is the problem of *ishut* in our time. We are faced with a problem of intermarriage unprecedented in Jewish history and with the children born of such unions. How can we retrieve some of them for Jewish life? If we only follow the *halachah*—that the child of a Jewish mother is Jewish—we declare that more than half of the children of such unions are not Jewish since more Jewish men marry non-Jewish women than vice versa. Since patrilineal is biblical and since in rabbinic terms matrilineal, why can't we return to patrilineal descent as well?

Our role as rabbis—Reform rabbis or otherwise—is to do for our generation what Moses did for his and Joshua for his and the rabbis for each of their generations. We hope by our study of the past and our confrontation with the present to show that we too are filled with the spirit of wisdom, which as Ibn Ezra said, is another name for the spirit of God.

˙I am grateful to Rabbis Leonard Kravitz and A. Stanley Dreyfus for their helpful suggestions in the preparation of this paper.

THE ORIGINS OF ORDINATION

LAWRENCE A. HOFFMAN

The topic of ordination in tannaitic Palestine is ideal for scholarly debate. The data are sufficiently inconclusive as to be potentially supportive of endless speculation and thus apt to germinate enough discussion to support generations of scholars for years to come. One researcher, for example, notes the utter impossibility of uncovering "*ein deutliches Bild*" [a clear picture].[1] And another concludes with the apology that when all is said and done, he cannot produce direct evidence to prove the veracity of his interpretation.[2]

My goal here, then, is to provide more than just another reconstruction of the evidence. I want to make the entire debate available to English readers by isolating pivotal questions, summarizing alternative solutions available in the secondary literature, and citing, translating, and analyzing anew the primary sources on which these hypotheses rest. Finally, I shall state my own tentative conclusions, which will emphasize the dubious validity of any detailed theory of the topic, and also the reasons why our data should be such as to be supportive of only possible hypotheses, not certain truths.

The following issues will be isolated for separate consideration:

1. *The laying on of hands.* We wish to know if this was ever part of the classical Jewish ordination ceremony. If so, was there, to speak very loosely, any sort of sacramental quality associated with the practice? Finally, was the custom abandoned, and if so, when and why?

2. *Stages of development.* The sources indicate three distinct developments in the ordination procedure. The first, marked by individual rabbis ordaining their disciples, I shall call the Personal Period. The second, in which the Patriarch alone is said to have awarded ordination, I shall label the Period of Centralization. Finally, we are told that the Patriarch and rabbis representative of the Scholar Class generally together ordained candidates; this I call the Compromise Period. Our task here is to delineate the chronological boundaries of each period, and to explain the reasons behind the changes from period to period.

3. *The liturgical ceremony.* Other than the laying on of hands, claims for or against six specific ceremonials have been made:

 a. a liturgical formulary announcement
 b. special garb for the ordinand
 c. a public response by those in attendance
 d. a speech by the ordinee
 e. the recording in a register of the ordinee's name; or, alternatively, the awarding of a letter of validation.
 f. the regulation that there be at least three people in the ordaining company

4. *Terminology.* We shall see that the key to these conundrums is semantic.

71

Specifically, we will have to analyze the use of the two Hebrew words, *smkh* and *mnh* (and their Aramaic equivalents) in Palestinian and Babylonian sources, asking what terms were preferred when, where, and in what contexts.

Two preliminary caveats are in order before beginning this analysis. It should be noted that an exhaustive study of every related issue would expand this paper beyond all reasonable length, so I have had to pass over such interesting topics as the function of ordained rabbis, the Sanhedrin, Jewish law relating to fines and calendration, and the role of the Elders, even though these subjects fall within the time frame which concerns us. Similarly I have only sketched developments after 200, such as the limiting of ordination to Palestine, the cessation of ordination, and attempts to reestablish it. Where the development of my thesis required my touching on these matters, of course, I dealt with them sufficiently to define the issues, to indicate their significance for us, and (in footnote form) to point to some relevant bibliography.

My second apologia is that I have deliberately omitted from consideration any evidence from non-rabbinic sources. What we have here is that which can fairly be concluded from what the rabbis themselves said about what they did. So my final conclusions are rooted in these sources alone and may justly be criticized on the basis of evidence gleaned elsewhere.

1. *Laying on of Hands*

Despite almost complete scholarly consensus that early Jewish ordination included the laying on of hands, the custom "cannot be proved either way from all our rabbinical literature."[3] The clear indication that Moses "ordained" Joshua this way (Num. 27:22-23, Deut. 34:9) is sometimes taken incorrectly as sufficient evidence to establish a parallel rabbinic custom.[4] But this is pure speculation based on the assumption that the rabbinic use of the verb *smkh* (and its nominal form, *semikhah*) is the semantic equivalent of the term as it appears in the biblical example of Moses and Joshua. Those who make this claim cite, at most, six sources (some with several recensions) to substantiate their position; each deserves separate consideration.

a. P. T. Yoma 1:1 = Meg. 1:10 reads:

הכהן במה הוא מתמנה רבנן דקיסרין בשם ר׳ חייא בר יוסף בפה אמר ר׳ זעירה הדא
אמרה שממנין זקנים בפה

> How is a priest appointed? Our rabbis of Caesarea in the name of Hiyya bar Jacob said, "By mouth." Said R. Zeira, "That implies that they appoint elders by mouth."

It is hard to imagine what support this source could lend to those arguing for the laying on of hands. It stipulates oral proclamation without even mentioning *semikhah*. Nevertheless, at least two scholars derive the lesson that the laying on of hands must still have been practiced in R. Zeira's time (circa 280).[5] I would argue, on the contrary, that we have yet to prove that it was ever in existence; that the whole debate was academic anyway since priests and elders had ceased by Zeira's day; and that to argue for the laying on of hands from a source that speaks only of proclamation is hardly valid at any rate.

b. In B. San. 13b we read:

אמר ליה רב אחא בריה דרבא לרב אשי׃ בידא ממש סמכין ליה אמר ליה סמכין ליה
בשמא קרי ליה רבי ויהבי ליה רשותא למידן דיני קנסות

Rav Acha the son of Raba asked Rav Ashi, "Do they ordain with hands,
literally?" He responded, "They ordain by naming, they call him 'Rabbi,' and
they give him the right to adjudicate cases involving fines."

To be sure, the notion of laying on of hands is at least mentioned here, even if
it is rejected. Still, it is argued that this very rejection must presuppose an
original practice no longer in existence; thus, though no longer the custom in
Rav Ashi's day (d. 425), the laying on of hands had been usual some time
previously.[6] On the other hand, the Hebrew *semikhah* or the Aramaic equivalent *semikhuta* that is used throughout the Babli for "ordination" is the very
same word utilized by both the Bible and the Mishnah for laying one's hands on
an offering. Hence one might argue that R. Acha's question was academic, i.e.,
"Do we really use our hands to ordain, as we do to sacrifice?" Neither sacrifice
nor (as we shall see) ordination was practiced in Rav Acha's Babylonia. The
question was academic then, hardly substantive. But even if this be denied, it
seems difficult to postulate the existence of a custom from a source that
categorically denies it.

c. How normally perspicacious scholars could misuse the above evidence is
worth a moment's consideration. It may well be that they were conditioned to
see the laying on of hands by their familiarity with medieval Jewish traditions
which postulated its existence at an earlier time. Though Jewish tradition is by
no means unanimous on the matter, we do find Isaac of Barcelona (eleventh
century) stating explicitly that it was once practiced, and several late *midrashim* speculate about such things as passing on the spirit by laying one's hand
on a disciple.[7] But medieval assumptions about ancient practices are not very
reliable, particularly here, where the word *semikhah* may have set off the same
semantic association as that which prompted the question to Rav Ashi.
Moreover, none of these writers quote older supportive material known to them
but not to us. Their speculations were based on the same tannaitic and amoraic
literature under analysis here, and there is no reason to believe that their ability
to reconstruct actual historical processes from these sparse reports was any
better than ours.

d. More to the point is evidence from tannaitic sources themselves. A much-
debated passage in this regard is M. Hagigah 2:2:

יוסי בן יועזר אומר שלא לסמוך יוסי בן יוחנן אומר לסמוך. יהושע בן פרחיה אומר
שלא לסמוך נתאי הארבלי אומר לסמוך. יהודה בן טבאי אומר שלא לסמוך שמעון בן
שטח אומר לסמוך. שמעיה אומר לסמוך אבטליון אומר שלא לסמוך. הלל ומנחם לא
נחלקו. יצא מנחם, נכנס שמאי. שמאי אומר שלא לסמוך הלל אומר לסמוך.
הראשונים היו נשיאים, והשניים להם אבות בית דין.

Five successive Pairs are cited here in an apparently century-long feud over
whether *lismokh* or *lo' lismokh*. But do they mean here by *semikhah* the laying

on of hands in ordination? Or are they discussing the laying of hands on a sacrifice?

From the middle of the nineteenth century a veritable battery of scholars have opted for ordination as the subject matter, on the grounds that, in the words of one of their number:

> Die Forscher der neuesten Zeit . . . finden es höchst auffallend, dass eine Controverse über das "Handauflegen" bei den Opfern . . . so lange beschäftigt hätte—durch einen Zeitraum von mehreren Generationen. Sie gelangen daher zu der Annahme, dass in Hintergrund der Controverse wichtige Momente oder Principien verborgen sind.[8]

The assumption that the proper conduct of the sacrificial cult is not a significant matter is a bias peculiar to modern scholars. Cultic regulations are probably the most prominent feature both of Mosaic regulations and of tannaitic discussions. Indeed, either Jews in the days of the Temple's existence took their worship seriously or they did not; and if they did, why should they not have debated the proper means of sacrificing? Moreover, in this case anyway, the context clearly indicates that the issue is a sacrifice. Our passage comes immediately after it explicitly stipulates a debate between the Hillelites and the Shammaites over the laying of hands on whole offerings.[9] Finally, the parallel passage in the Tosefta is construed by some as evidence in favor of the cultic interpretation. Though the Tosefta support is not as clear-cut as the proponents of the sacrificial interpretation would have it,[10] the burden of proof falls on those who would select ordination as the true interpretation; not the other way around.

This is the case on linguistic grounds alone. In the entire Mishnah, variants of the word *smkh* appear roughly 150 times.[11] The word is used in a variety of senses, including dependence on,[12] physical abutment,[13] and sacrifice. References to sacrificial hand-laying are extremely numerous.[14] But nowhere do we find the word used for ordination.[15] The decision to relate the word here to ordination is simply unsubstantiated by anything but a bias against debate on sacrifice, and a corresponding preference for such "wichtige Momente oder Principien" as ordination suggests to the modern Western mind.

I would, without hesitation, conclude with Albeck: "The word *semikhah* by itself in the Mishnah refers to *semikhah* on the sacrifice . . . [and] cannot be interpreted in the sense of ordination of sages";[16] and with Lieberman, who analyzes the evidence with thoroughness and precision, concludes that the sense here is doubtlessly sacrificial, and summarizes, "How many scholars of our day want to relate *semikhah* to another context! But there is absolutely no foundation for their words."[17]

e. The only other case in the Mishnah in which *smkh* is taken by some to refer to ordination is Sanhedrin 4:4. Regarding the Sanhedrin, we are told:

ושלש שורות של תלמידי חכמים יושבים לפניהם כל אחד ואחד מכיר את מקומו היו
צריכין לסמוך סומכין מן הראשונה.

Three rows of sages sat before them. Each one knew his place; if they needed to *smkh*, they did so, starting with the first.

Bacher, for example, takes this as an obvious case of ordination.[18] It should be noted, however, that even if this is ordination, the sense of the report hardly suggests the ceremonial laying on of hands. Moreover, the text is a continuation of M. San. 4:3, which begins, "There used to be a Sanhedrin . . .," so we have here a very late post-facto account of what some Tannaim thought once was the case; but which may not correspond to reality at all. Finally, the assumption that selection as a member of the Sanhedrin was tantamount to receiving ordination is itself without foundation. Indeed, our very text itself indicates that the candidates from among whom the new member was selected were already *talmidei chakhamim*, and a Tosefta passage indicates that this category of "sages" had already received ordination.[19]

Nevertheless, we must make some sense out of the use of *smkh* in this passage. Albeck thinks it means simply, "selection, in the sense that they selected an elder who was already ordained to be a member of the Sanhedrin."[20] Albeck is correct, but Sidon came closest to explaining the use of *smkh* in this instance. Arguing directly with Bacher, he adduced the Tosefta description of adding to one's tithe, pointing out that the word for "adding" there is *smkh*, and thus: "darunter (San. 4:4) gemeint sein kann, dass sie ergänzt wurden, wenn es nöthig war."[21] That is to say, our Sanhedrin citation merely means that the number of members was supplemented, or added to, when necessary. It is an extension of the denotation of physical abutment to the related case of personal adjoining. Here too then, even if the report be true, the verb *smkh* in no way implies ordination, much less the laying on of hands.

Only one more source remains, and since it deals directly with the question of whether three people were required for ordination, I will postpone considering it until the proper place. But there too I shall argue that those who take *semikhah* to be ordination are plainly mistaken. Assuming in advance the validity of that argument, we would have to conclude our investigation into the laying on of hands at ordination by saying:

1. There is no evidence whatever of the custom in tannaitic literature, i.e., preceding the year 200.
2. The amoraic sources (i.e., the next several centuries) consist of (a) a report by R. Zeira describing "proclamation" but completely silent regarding the laying on of hands, and (b) a statement in which Rav Ashi expressly denies that laying on of hands was practiced.
3. There was, therefore, never any laying on of hands.[22] How the mistaken notion that it was practiced should have become prevalent despite the absence of evidence is a matter to which we shall return at the end of our analysis.

I indicated at the beginning that I would discuss the scholarly debate on any sacramentalism (loosely conceived) that might have inhered in the practice of laying on of hands. To be sure, if there never was any laying on of hands, the issue is moot. To debate the presumed significance of a custom that never existed is surely the height of nonsense. Still, in the event that I am wrong, I should at least record the fact that there are researchers who seem to believe that in the laying on of hands, Jews in the tannaitic period understood an event to be occurring that we might classify as sacramental. Thus, for example, Newman, Dinabourg [Dinur], and Rothkoff all stress the biblical paradigm of Moses and Joshua, and indicate that the hands are the instrument by which the spirit of Moses was passed on.[23] Even Baron says that Palestinian ordination bore "almost a sacred character."[24] Others, particularly Gaster, take the opposite view, that "Jewish ordination does not partake of a sacerdotal or sacramental character."[25] It should be emphasized that these opinions are nowhere substantiated by anything that first- or second-century Jewish literature has to say. The only citations given are the Bible and then medieval homiletical statements.[26] That sacramentalism per se was not beyond or alien to the Jewish community in question I do not doubt. But in the case of their laying on of hands there is no evidence, since we can hardly expect Jews at the time to have told us what they thought about something they did not do!

The debate over the sacramental quality of the laying on of hands during ordination is really a thinly disguised debate over presumptive models intended to serve as an explanatory hermeneutic for the inner workings of Jewish ceremonial in the formative tannaitic period. At best, the debate is a "meta-debate" not on the evidence (which does not even exist) but on what such evidence might be construed as implying about Jewish spirituality. As such it is really not part of our topic at all.

2. *Stages of Development*

Two basic sources indicate that the history of ordination may be divided into three different periods.

> א״ר בא בראשונה היה כל אחד ואחד ממנה את תלמידיו, כגון רבן יוחנן בן זכיי מינה
> את רבי ליעזר ואת רבי יהושע, ורבי יהושע את רבי עקיבא, ורבי עקיבא את רבי
> מאיר ואת רבי שמעון. חזרו וחלקו כבוד לבית הזה. אמרו בית דין שמינה שלא לדעת
> הנשיא אין מינויו מינוי. ונשיא שמינה שלא לדעת בית מינויו מינוי. חזרו והתקינו
> שלא יהו ב״ד ממנין אלא מדעת הנשיא. ושלא יהא הנשיא ממנה אלא מדעת ב״ד
> (ירוש׳ סנ׳ י״ט א׳).

(A) Rabbi Ba said, "Originally, everyone used to ordain his own students. For example, Rabban Yochanan ben Zakkai ordained Rabbi Lazar and Rabbi Joshua; Rabbi Joshua [ordained] Rabbi Akiba; and Rabbi Akiba [ordained] Rabbi Meir and Rabbi Simeon. . . . They changed matters and rendered honor to this dynasty [lit: house, i.e., the House of David, which had held the Patriarchate virtually the whole tannaitic period]. They said, 'If the court ordains without the concurrence of the Patriarch, the ordination is invalid; if the Patriarch ordains without the concurrence of the court, the ordination is valid.' Then they changed and ruled that the court should not ordain without the concurrence of the Patriarch, and the Patriarch should not ordain without the concurrence of the court.[27]

> פעם אחת גזרה מלכות הרשעה גזירה על ישראל שכל הסומך יהרג וכל הנסמך יהרג
> ועיר שסומכין בה תיחרב ותחומין שסומכין בהן יעקרו. מה עשה יהודה בן בבא הלך
> וישב לו בין שני הרים גדולים ובין שתי עיירות גדולות ובין שני תחומי שבת בין
> אושא לשפרעם וסמך שם חמשה זקנים ואלו הן ר״מ ור׳ יהודה ור׳ שמעון ור׳ יוסי
> ור׳ אלעזר בן שמוע. רב אויא מוסיף אף ר׳ נחמיה. כיון שהכירו אויביהם בהן אמר
> להן בניי רוצו. אמרו לו רבי מה תהא עליך אמר להן הריני מוטל לפניהם כאבן שאין
> לה הופכים.
>
> אחריני הוו בהדיה והאי דלא חשיב להו משום כבודו דרבי יהודא בן בבא.

(B) Once the evil kingdom [Rome] passed a regulation against Israel: anyone who ordained would be killed; anyone who was ordained would be killed; a city in which ordination occurred would be destroyed, and the boundaries in which it took place uprooted. What did Judah ben Bava do? He went between two large mountains . . . and there ordained five Elders: R. Meir, R. Judah, R. Simeon, R. Yose, and R. Elazar ben Shammua. Rav Avya added, "Also R. Nehemiah." As soon as their enemies recognized them, he [R. Judah ben Bava] said to them, "Run, my sons!" "What will happen to you, Rabbi," they asked. He responded, "I will lie before them like a stone which no one [bothers to] overturn." [The report goes on to say how R. Judah ben Bava was martyred, and then] other people were with him [when he ordained these people] but the reason that they are not mentioned is in honor of R. Judah ben Bava.[28]

Account A divides the periods into what I have called Personal, Centralization, and Compromise, and Account B describes what may have been a Personal ordination under the difficult conditions that obtained during the Hadrianic persecutions occasioned by the Bar Kokhba revolt. It may indeed have been the last such instance. Though there is no way of knowing when this Personal Period began, there is reason to believe it ended with the ban issued by Hadrian.[29] If there was any laying on of hands, it would have coincided with this period, after which it was replaced with ordination by proclamation.[30]

Account A continues to describe the period I have called Centralization; that is, when the Patriarch alone could ordain, but the other rabbis could not. Since this period must postdate the description contained in the first part of A—that is, the ordination of R. Meir and R. Simeon by R. Akiba—the *terminus a quo* for the change is the Bar Kokhba revolt. Precisely when, however? There are stories aplenty of Judah I ruling in an iron manner, and even instructing his son on his deathbed how to go about ordaining.[31] So the *terminus ad quem* would seem to be the death of Judah I (circa 200). Therefore, some time between 135 and 200, under either Judah I or his predecessor, Simon ben Gamaliel II (140–165), the Centralization Period began. Scholarly opinion is divided between the two. Graetz and Chajes, for example, support Judah; Bacher, Dinabourg [Dinur], and Newman favor Simon.[32]

As hard as it is to determine when Centralization began, it is harder still to ascertain when it ended. To be sure, tantalizing anecdotes—or, more frequently, mere remnants of anecdotes—carried in amoraic literature shed some light on the relationship between the Patriarch and the scholar class, but that relationship is nowhere described in nearly enough detail for us to infer a specific date when the compromise between the hitherto prominent Patriarch and his colleagues of the Court necessarily occurred.

This time there are no fewer than five candidates, Judah I and his successors: Gamaliel III (210–230), Judah II (230–286), Gamaliel IV, and Judah III (286–330).[33] Since the changeover to Compromise is beyond the time confines of this paper, further discussion need not detain us. The reason behind the compromise, however, is worth noting. At issue is the alleged misuse of ordination by the Patriarch. Talmudic literature charges him with corruption, nepotism, and outright simony.[34] We are witness to a third-century struggle for authority between the Patriarch, who had once commanded sufficient power to achieve autonomous control over rabbinic appointments, and the scholar class, which now reasserted its right to share in the decision-making process. Evidence from the Talmud regarding patriarchal malfeasance should be viewed as politically biased information; and the compromise between the two parties, whenever it occurred, should in no way be misconstrued as a victory of good (the rabbis) over evil (the Patriarch).[35]

This third state too eventually ended. By the thirteenth century, if not earlier, it was widely assumed (a) that ordination was possible only in Palestine; and (2) that it had ceased there. The exact point of its cessation is, as Newman describes it, "the most obscure problem of our subject,"[36] and, fortunately, well beyond the scope of our investigation here. Suffice it to say that the terminal date has been variously set anywhere from the Patriarch Hillel II (mid-fourth century) to Maimonides (d. 1204).[37]

3. Ceremony

We have already discussed the laying on of hands. We may now profitably turn to other ceremonial actions which are purported to have occurred as part of the ordination rite in the tannaitic period.

(a) Formulary Announcement

We noted above that both R. Zeira and Rav Ashi knew of some verbal means by which ordination was granted. The former described it as being בפה, "by mouth," meaning, perhaps, by proclamation. The latter thought candidates were called by name, given the title "Rabbi" and the right to adjudicate cases of *kenas*, or fines. R. Zeira and Rav Ashi were Amoraim, however, living after the period which interests us. Their laconic statements are open to interpretation in any case, but even if they mean what they seem to mean, and if they are correct for their day, the validity of their recollection for tannaitic Palestine is still far from certain.

But popular wisdom on the subject adds yet another claim for some kind of verbal bestowal of authority, this one based on an incident in the time of Judah I. We are told of two students, Rav and Rabbah bar Hana, who were emigrating from Palestine to Babylonia.

כי הוה נחית רבה בר חנה בר חנה לבבל אמר ליה רבי חייא לרבי בן אחי יורד לבבל יורה יורה
ידין ידין יתיר בכורות יתיר כי הוה נחית רב לבבל אמר ליה רבי חייא לר׳ בן אחותי
יורד לבבל יורה יורה ידין ידין יתיר בכורות אל יתיר.

When Rabbah bar Hana went to Babylon, Rabbi Hiyya said to Rabbi [Judah I]: My nephew is going to Babylonia. *yoreh yoreh yadin yadin yatir bekhorot yatir.* . . . When Rav emigrated to Babylonia, R. Hiyya asked Rabbi [Judah I]: *yoreh yoreh yadin yadin yatir bekhorot 'al yatir.*[38]

I leave the Hebrew untranslated, as any translation presupposes the nature of the verbal interchange, and it is precisely its nature which is in question. What seems clear is that the three verbs, *yoreh*, *yadin*, and *yatir*, represent different juridical duties for which specific authorization was required, though exactly what they were is open to question and beside the point in our discussion.[39] Our source, then, appears to be a conversation between R. Hiyya and the Patriarch, Judah I, over the extent of authority being granted the former's two nephews. The traditional punctuation converts the phrase into a series of questions by Hiyya and answers by Judah. Thus: (Hiyya:) May he "*yoreh*"? (Judah:) He may "*yoreh*." (Hiyya:) May he "*yadin*"? (Judah:) He may "*yadin*." And so on.

As I say, popular wisdom has converted this report of a conversation between the Patriarch and a rabbi into a formula for ordination. We are told, for example, "The complete formula was, *Yoreh, yoreh. Yadin yadin. Yatir yatir.* (May he decide? He may decide. May he judge? He may judge. May he permit? He may permit.)"[40]

This interpretation of our pericope seems to me to be highly speculative. It appears to be an official formula because (1) it is cited in the case of two rabbis, not just one, and (2) in both cases the wording is the same. But the report is deceptive. In actuality we have one story in which similar words are put in the mouths of R. Hiyya and Judah twice. The phrase occurs, after all, only in this one place; we never hear of it regarding the other rabbis who were ordained. What we have here is a stylized shorthand account of two presumed conversations in which the ordinand is not even present! Its purpose is to fill out the dialectic of a particular talmudic argument, and even though the conversations may well have occurred in some form or other, there was nothing liturgical about the context and nothing formulaic about the content. To conclude otherwise would be to confuse oral (and eventually, literary) stylization of an event for the event itself. So while logic would have it that something was said to ordinands on the occasion of their ordination, our sources give no indication of what, if anything, it was. And whether it was liturgical or not remains pure speculation.

(b) *Special Garb for the Ordinand.*

This issue is fully discussed by Newman.[41] In sum, there exist a variety of stories about special garments for ordinands. Most of the citations do not explictly mention ordination, however, and could be interpreted as referring to special status-signifying robes such as those worn by a judge in our courts today. On the other hand, such status indicators might very well have been displayed when the title which they marked was conferred. The following passage comes closest to supporting this contention.

אמר ר׳ ברכיה לזקן שהיתה לו מעפרת והיה מצוה את תלמידו ואומר לו קפלה ונערה ותן דעתך עליה. אמר לו אדוני זקן מכל מעפראות שיש לך אי אתה מצוה אותי אלא על זו?! אמר לו מפני שאותה לבשתי ביום שנתמניתי זקן.

R. Berechya [discussing the chosenness of Israel implicit in Lev. 1:1, where Moses is told to "Speak to the children of Israel," said] the matter is like an Elder who had a hood, and would order his student, saying, "Fold it and shake it out and take care of it." He asked, "My Lord the Elder, of all the hoods you own, you order me only about this one?" He responded, "That is because I wore it the day I was appointed an Elder."[42]

Now, in fact, though this passage does suggest the existence of a special ordination hood, it does not prove it. R. Berechya (fourth-generation Amora) is not discussing his own situation, but making up a story about a hypothetical Elder who wore a hood when he was appointed to his station. Whether there ever were Elders who wore hoods at their appointments is pure speculation. The narrator may have in mind nothing more unusual than an ordinary piece of clothing which the Elder happened to have on when he received his charge, and to which he has harbored fond sentiment ever since. My own guess, and we can do no more than guess, is that Jewish society in tannaitic times like many other societies in other eras, tended to mark official status with special uniforms, whether formally demanded or informally adopted. The status hierarchy was observable by the different kinds of clothes which were permissible. We cannot know now what those clothes were, or whether people wore them always or only at officiating circumstances. But different functionaries wore different designating garments. Whether they donned them at the moment when the status was conferred, that is, at the ceremony of appointment, depends on what that ceremony was like. Newman assumes that there was an elaborate ceremony; so the notion of some ancient equivalent to the contemporary custom of wearing clerical garb at ordination ceremonies makes sense for him. My argument thus far, however, has tended in the opposite direction. There was never any laying on of hands; we know of no formulary proclamation; and the levels of authority to which one might be appointed varied considerably, so that even if there was a major ceremony for one, there may not have been for others. Thus Newman may be right in arguing for a special ordination garb; or he may be right but only for specific as-yet-undifferentiated cases; or he may be wrong. The evidence is ambiguous.

(c) *Response.*

The only actual evidence of ceremonial comes from two reports of what appear to be public exclamations that accompanied the ordination of R. Zeira; and Rabbis Ammi and Assi. But the accounts are so truncated and their meaning so opaque, it is difficult to know what to do with them.

כי סמכוה לר׳ זירא שרו ליה הכי לא כחל ולא שרק ולא פירכוס ויעלת חן. כי סמכוה
לרבי אמי ולרבי אסי שרו להו הכי כל כל מן דין כל דין מן דין סמוכו לנא. לא תסמכו לנא
לא מסרמיטין ולא מסרמיסין ואמרי לה לא מחמיסין ולא מטורמיסין.

When they ordained R. Zeira, they sang to him: "No eye make-up, no rouge, no hair-do, but a graceful doe." When they ordained R. Ammi and R. Assi, they sang to them thus: "Only like these, only like these ordain for us. Do not ordain for us [unqualified scholars]."[43]

What we are to make of these reports is very hard to say. To complicate matters, we are elsewhere informed that R. Zeira's song was actually a Palestinian wedding song, sung for the bride,[44] and indeed, unlike the song for Ammi and Assi, one is at a loss to find any relevance between the words of Zeira's song and his ordination. So Newman states that he was probably ordained at his wedding.[45] But if so, the proper conclusion should be that we have here a wedding song which just happened to be sung at an ordination, not an ordination song, as Newman would have it. Ammi and Assi's song, on the other hand, does fit the ordination context, though it seems hardly a song, so much as a vocal political polemic by the rabbis against a "corrupt" Patriarch who appoints unfit candidates to office.[46]

Shall we, then, conclude that "after the ceremony the scholars present praised in rhythmic sentences the person ordained"?[47] Such a far-reaching conclusion seems to me highly tenuous. We know only that some people shouted approval in the case of Ammi and Assi, and that a wedding song somehow became attached to the tradition of R. Zeira's ordination. What makes these two entirely diverse cases seem like evidence of a pattern is the Babylonian Talmud's linking them together with similar editorial introductory phrases, i.e., "When they ordained X, they sang A; when they ordained Y, they sang B." To conclude from this that "whenever they ordained anyone, they sang something," is to confuse Babylonian editorial work for Palestinian actual practice; and to ignore entirely the way in which oral material arose, was carried, and later transmuted into stylized written accounts in the Gemara.[48]

(d) *Speech by the Ordinee*

Newman asserts that "a talmudical passage in Sanhedrin suggests that it had been a general rule that after the ceremony of the ordination the candidate delivered a public discourse on some talmudic subject."[49] The passage to which he alludes reads as follows:

דבי נשיאה אוקמו דיינא דלא הוה גמיר א״ל ליהודה בר נחמני מתורגמניה דריש
לקיש קום עליה באמורא קם גחין עליה ולא א״ל ולא מידי פתח ואמר הוי אומר לעץ
הקיצה עורי לאבן דומם הוא יורה . . . אמר ריש לקיש כל המעמיד דיין שאינו הגון
כאילו נוטע אשירה בישראל.

Members of the patriarchal household promoted an unlearned man as judge. They said to Judah bar Nachmani, the interpreter of Resh Lakish, "Get up and interpret for him." He got up and leaned over [to hear what he was saying] but he did not say anything. So Judah began the discourse [himself] saying, "Woe unto him who says 'Awake' to wood; 'Arise' to a dumb stone. Can such a one teach [*yoreh*]? . . . Resh Lakish said, "Appointing an unfit judge is like planting an *asherah* in Israel."[50]

I fail to see in this story any allusion whatever to ordination ceremonial. To begin with, the normal terms for ordination are not even present. We have neither *smkh* (the usual Babylonian phrase) nor *mnh* (the preferred Palestinian term). Instead we find the *'aphel* of *kum*, "they promoted, raised up," and the *hiphil* of *'md*, which amounts to the same thing. Secondly, there is nothing at all to suggest that the judge's speech was his first, or that it followed upon his "ordination," except for the imputed causal relationship between the patriarchal appointment of mediocrity and a judge's inability to give a speech. Surely what we have here is another antipatriarchal narrative, part of the third-century struggle for authority between Patriarch and rabbis which we have encountered all along. In this case the latter are represented by Resh Lakish, who makes the moral manifest by his singular conclusion that appointing unfit judges is tantamount to promoting idolatry. Even if the rabbis conspired to embarrass a judicial appointee of the Patriarch, the fact that the incident is tied in the final narrative to a patriarchal appointment in no way indicates that these two events followed chronologically, one immediately after the other. The speech could have been years after the appointment, for all we know, but the time lapse was omitted as unimportant to the narrator, who was making the political point of patriarchal malfeasance, symbolized in this case by a judge who could not speak.

(e) *A Register of Ordinees, or a Letter of Qualification*

Secondary literature contains a debate, principally between Bacher and Newman, on the existence of written testimony to the ordinees' status. I judge a full investigation into this controversy to be beyond the scope of this paper, since it elucidates neither the history nor the ceremony of ordination in any meaningful way. For the sake of completion, however, we should note the claims made on either side. Bacher maintains that a register of all ordinees along with the date of their ordination was kept in the Patriarch's office. This allowed him to apply a seniority rule in appointing people to the council charged with intercalating the calendar.[51] Newman argues that there was no written registry, but there was a letter of authority testifying to one's ordination and, since there were different degrees of ordination, to the specific duties one was qualified to perform.[52] I must confess that I find neither view sustantiated by the evidence. But even if a register and/or a letter of authority were granted to official appointees, this would not necessarily imply anything beyond the fact that people appointed to public office had their credentials duly recorded. We do not necessarily learn anything about ordination from this fact, if indeed it is a fact to start with.

(f) *The Necessity for Three Elders*

The belief that ordination required a minimum of three is almost universally held. Rothkoff, for example, simply says so categorically,[53] and Kasovsky translates certain mishnaic passages as attesting to this fact.[54] These modern scholars echo practically the totality of Jewish tradition on the subject. The tenth-century Babylonian savant, Sherira, was of that opinion, and he was recorded in the 'Arukh, whose eleventh-century editor believed him.[55] Roughly a century later, Maimonides concurred without debate, possibly depending on a tradition handed down by the tenth-century Rabbenu Hananel.[56]

This well-nigh universal opinion is based on a tannaitic phrase סמיכת זקנים בשלשה, or, as it appears elsewhere, סמיכות זקנים בשלשה.[57] *Zekenim* is clearly "Elders," and *sheloshah* is clearly "three," the required minimum number. But what is *semikhat*. The general opinion adduced above takes *semikhat* to refer to ordination. The passage thus becomes, "The ordination of Elders requires three [Elders]."

This position is then left with the problem of explaining why the requirement for three arose, especially as there is no known description of ordination with three people in all of tannaitic and amoraic literature. Indeed there is one case at least, that of Judah ben Bava (San. 14a) cited above, where clearly Judah ordained alone. True, the Babli suggests that others were really present, and that their names were withheld out of deference to Judah. But that response is just one side of the dialectical argumentation typical of talmudic debate. Party One has suggested we need three; Party Two has correctly cited the case of Judah to show we do not; so Party One responds with the suggestion that perhaps others really were there, but anonymously. Even those who favor the notion of a quorum of three generally admit that this talmudic response to the precedent of Judah cannot be taken seriously.[58]

Any serious solution must allow for Judah ben Bava's ordaining without two other colleagues present, so it is argued that Judah's individual action typified the Personal Period, and that the law demanding three came later. The most logical time for such a development would be the Compromise Period, when, perhaps, the Patriarch along with two rabbinic representatives (the *'av bet din* and the *chakham* were two known positions of this class during the time of Judah II) ordained together. Scholars therefore usually advocate dates dependent on their stand regarding the changeover from Centralization to Compromise.

I shall later refer to this approach to ordination as the Developmental Model. It explains contrary data by assigning them to different times. In this case, we save both the Personal Period, with Judah ben Bava's example of solitary heroism, and the idea that ordination requires three people by assuming that the latter situation developed from the former. Unfortunately, the application of the Developmental Model here creates more difficulties than it solves.

Bornstein, for example, is content to call the quorum of three "a late development." His reasoning is telling. It must be late, he argues, because the Mishnah allots considerable space to listing things which require three people, and ordination is not among them! So Bornstein explains its absence by assuming that the law never existed in pre-200 times. [59] To this, Newman objects that Bornstein gives neither a date nor a reason why the new law should have been adopted, and avers that it must have occurred "between the time of Gamaliel II and R. Judah Nessiah II," because by then the law had been formulated in the Tosefta, and "had long taken root." [60] Why the Tosefta should have formulated the law in the first place is unclear, as is the reason why it should have "taken root" despite the Mishnah and all past precedent. This objection is behind Albeck's analysis. He concludes that the new regulation reflected the changeover from Centralization to Compromise. But the new law is in the Tosefta, so it cannot be dated beyond the early third century. The rule must therefore have been in effect by the time R. Yochanan and R. Joshua b. Levi reached maturity (mid-third century). Yet there are instances in our sources where these two rabbis ordain by themselves, despite the compromise rule requiring the Patriarch's assent, and, apparently, in breach of the rule requiring three. So he is led to conclude that individuals did indeed ordain privately even in the Compromise Period, but that in order for these ordinees to get placed in positions they required the Patriarch's presence. The Rule of Three then was a practical requirement for men seeking community positions. [61]

With all of these difficulties we certainly have the right, if not the obligation, to analyze each instance of the troublesome phrase *semikhat* (or *semikhut*) *zekenim bisheloshah* to see whether in fact it really meant ordination in the first place. Since in our discussion of the laying on of hands we saw that *semikhah*, when used in tannaitic sources, referred only to sacrificial matters, we might well suspect that here too the phrase means simply, "The laying of the Elders' hands [on the sacrifice] requires three [Elders]." Particularly does this seem logical when we consider the fact that Lev. 4:13-15 knows of a unique sacrifice in which,

> If the whole congregation of Israel shall err. . . . The assembly shall offer a young bullock as a sin-offering, and bring it before the tent of meeting. Then the

elders of the congregation *shall lay their hands* on the head of the bullock before
the Lord, and slaughter the bullock before the Lord.

Could it be that *semikhat zekenim* is not the ordination of the Elders at all, but
the laying of the Elders' hands on this bullock?

Again, only a careful look at each of the instances in which the phrase is used
will reveal its intent.[62]

(a) M. San. 1:3: סמיכת הזקנים ועריפת העגלה בשלשה—*Semikhat zekenim* and
the breaking of the heifer's neck require three.

If our phrase were to mean ordination, this would be the logical place for the
Mishnah to list it, as this is the central location where items are divided
according to the number of people required to do them.[63] But the pairing of
semikhat zekenim with the breaking of the heifer's neck suggests that both acts
are communal atonement rites. They are mentioned in one breath precisely
because the community Elders perform them both. We have already cited the
semikhat zekenim of Lev. 4:13-15, in which Elders lay their hands on a bullock
and then slaughter it to atone for a congregational sin. The breaking of the
heifer's neck is an exact parallel. (1) We deal with a corpse found near the city,
the murderer unknown, and the guilt, therefore, falling on the community as a
whole. (2) The city's Elders are required to "wash their hands over the heifer
whose neck was broken," and to attain divine pardon for the community.[64]

There is no reason to assume that this instance of *semikhat zekenim* is
ordination. Rather, it seems obvious that we have here one of two atonement
rites effected by the Elders, and paired together in the Mishnah as twin
instances in which three Elders are the required minimum.

(b) T. San. 1:1: סמיכה בשלשה וסמיכות זקנים בשלשה ר' יהודה אומ' בחמשה —
Semikhah requires three, and *semikhut* [or *semikhot*] *zekenim* requires three.

This is the regulation which Bornstein, Newman, and Albeck take as
ordination. (As we saw, this assumption led them to numerous secondary
difficulties.)[65] But except for prior conditioning, there is no reason to take either
semikhah or *semikhut* (or *semikhot*) *zekenim* here as anything but sacrificial in
intent. We have already quoted Albeck's contention that "the word *semikhah*
by itself in the Mishnah refers to *semikhah* on the sacrifice . . . and cannot be
interpreted in the sense of ordination."[66] Why should this not be true also of the
Tosefta, it too being a tannaitic work, especially since in our discussion of the
laying on of hands we surveyed Kasovsky's entries of the root *smkh* in the
Tosefta and in the Mishnah alike and found no instances whatever where
ordination was intended; except, of course, the disputed cases discussed here.

Semikhah is the act by which an individual puts his own hands on the
sacrifice, and the Mishnah allots considerable space to determining which
individuals put their hands on which offerings.[67] *Semikhat zekenim* is a
specialized case in which the identity of the sinner is unknown and the Elders
act on behalf of the corporate community. We are told here that both require the
presence of three.

What undoubtedly suggests to some people that Tosefta San. 1:1 (here)
differs from M. San. 1:3 (case [a] above), is: (a) the abstract noun *semikhut*
seems to parallel our English word "ordination" and its counterparts in the
modern European languages; and (b) the Palestinian Talmud actually says that

semikhah is not the same as *semikhut*.[68] As for (a), it should be objected that: (i) manuscripts of tannaitic literature frequently vary between *semikhut* and *semikhat*,[69] so we should not assume that what appears so important to the modern grammatical mind was equally significant for the Tannaim and medieval copiers of manuscripts; and (ii) the abstract noun *semikhut* may equally well be *semikhot*, the plural of *semikhah*, that is, "the laying on of hands," a description of the Elders, one after the other, laying their hands on the offering. That this was the actual practice we shall see from our next passage, T. Men. 10:15. As for (b) it should be objected that the amoraic differentiation between *semikhah* and *semikhut* (or *semikhot*) is just that, an amoraic distinction introduced to maintain one side of an academic argument against the other. This too we shall look at, and see that the anonymous amoraic statement is nothing but an editorial device utilized to sustain the hypothetical discussion.

In sum, the identification of *semikhut zekenim* as ordination of Elders depends upon a prior willingness to see it as such, supported perhaps by passages in T. Men 10:15 and P.T. San. 19a; to which we now turn.

(יב) כיצד סומך זבח . . . מניח שתי ידיו על גבי קרניו של זבח ולא היה מניח ידיו על
גבי זבח ולא היה מניח ידיו זו על גבי זו ולא היה דבר חוצץ בין ידים לקרנות מתודה
עליו . . .

(יג) סמיכה נוהגת בכהנים לוים וישראלים . . . אין נוהג לא בגוים ולא בנשים ולא
בעבדים ולא בקטנים.

(יד) חמשה שהביאו זבח אחד כולן סומכין עליו ולא כולן כאחד סומכין עליו אלא כל
אחד ואחד סומך ומסתלק.

(טו) סמיכה בשלשה סמיכת זקנים בשלשה ר' יהודה אומר בחמשה לא כולן כאחד
סומכין עליו אלא כל אחד ואחד סומך ומסתלק. איל המילואים אהרון ובניו כאחד.
תני הסמיכו' בשלש'. לא סמיכה היא סמיכות. תמן קריי למנוייה סמיכותא.

(c) *T. Men. 10:15. Semikhah bisheloshah semikhat zekenim bisheloshah.* I have included a larger sampling of the text, so as to indicate the context. We have an extended discussion of sacrificial acts like waving, laying on of hands, and actual slaughtering. In 10:12 we are told how *semikhah* is done, that is, two hands are placed separately on the animal's two horns. The social groups who may not perform *semikhah* (non-Jews, women, slaves, and minors) are enumerated in 10:13. Then (10:14) we come to the most significant case for our purposes, that in which five people bring one offering which they own jointly. They are to take turns putting their hands on it. Now we come to 10:15:

> *Semikhah* requires three; *semikhat zekenim* requires three; R. Judah says,
> "Five." The people do not put their hands on all at one time, but in turns, each
> putting his hands on and then stepping back. But with regard to the ram of
> consecration ['eil milu'im, cited in Ex. 29:23][70] Aaron and his sons lay their
> hands on together.

A full analysis of this Tosefta chapter is a separate paper unto itself. It seems, however, to be a composite text. The first sentence of the citation from 10:15 is part of another debate, irrelevant here, between two second-century Tannaim, Judah and Simeon, living more than half a century after the demise of the cultic events which they are discussing.[71] The second and third sentences (beginning *lo'kulan*) are continuations of the topic in 10:14, that is, whether people lay their hands all together on offerings or whether they take turns.

For our purposes, two observations are in order. (1) The disputed term *semikhat zekenim* occurs both here and in its original context from which it is borrowed[72] to refer to sacrifice. The information given parallels precisely T. San. 1:1 (b) above, *semikhut* (or *semikhot*) *zekenim* there being the same as *semikhat zekenim* here;[73] both say that *semikhah* and *semikhat zekenim* require three. (2) The second sentence and Men. 10:14 indicate that when many people laid their hands on a sacrifice, they did so one after the other. This may be reason to read T. San. 1:1 (b) not as *semikhut* but *semikhot*, the plural of *semikhah*, as suggested above. Alternatively, we have a mere difference in recension of no consequence, as the variant manuscript readings alluded to above indicate.[74]

(d) P.T. San. 19a. *Semikhat zekenim* and the breaking of the heifer's neck require three, according to R. Simeon; R. Judah says, "Five." [The discussion continues with the exegetical difference between the two, concerning their understanding of Lev. 4:15, the case of the Elders' sacrifice, and Deut. 21:2, the case of the heifer. Then] . . . it was taught in a *baraita:* תני הסמיכו' בשלש'.לא אסמיכותא למנוייה קריי תמן סמיכות. היא סמיכה סמיכה—*semikhut* requires three [thus supporting Simeon. But supporters of Judah might reply] *semikhut* is not the same as *semikhah*. In Babylonia [lit. over there] they call appointment [*minuy*] ordination [*semikhuta'*].[75]

Here we are supplied with two anonymous amoraic statements: (1) that *semikhut* is not the same as *semikhah;* and then (2) that *minuy*, or appointment, is called *semikhuta'*, or ordination, in Babylonia. This latter sentence leads to the source for dividing *minuy* into three periods. This whole debate was edited by people living after the Compromise Period began.

What we have here are two separate subjects telescoped into one. Beginning with the familiar debate regarding the Elders' sacrifice and the red heifer (the Mishnah under discussion), we have a lengthy argument on who is right, Simeon or Judah, and how each arrives at his opinion. A tannaitic statement is now adduced to support Simeon, i.e., "*semikhut* requires three." An anonymous Amora tries to defend Judah by refuting the validity of this new tannaitic statement: "*Semikhut* is not the same as *semikhah*." The discussion ends here. There is no reason to believe that the last speaker believed *semikhut* to be ordination.

The second discussion is a separate pericope about *minuy*, appointment. It has nothing whatever to do with the first discussion, but the editor has added a bridge between the two discussions to the effect that *semikhuta'* in Babylonia is *minuy* in Palestine. Thus the discussion can move from *semikhah* (in sacrifice) to *semikhuta'* (the term for ordination in Babylonia) to *minuy* (the parallel term in Palestine).[76]

In sum, the crucial phase, "*semikhut* is not the same as *semikhah*" need not be interpreted to mean that the Amora who said it thought that *semikhut* was ordination; or, in the unlikely event that he did, that he knew what he was talking about, since he knew full well that in Palestine ordination was never called *semikhah* but *minuy;* and the quotation in question was tannaitic and therefore Palestinian.

Finally, we turn to the last text, B. San 13b.

תנא סמיכה וסמיכת זקנים בג' מאי סמיכה ומאי סמיכת זקנים א"ר יוחנן מיסמך סבי א"ל אביי
לרב יוסף מיסמך סבי בשלשה מנלן אילימא מדכתיב ויסמוך את ידיו עליו אי הכי תסגי בחד וכי
תימא משה במקום שבעים וחד קאי אי הכי ליבעי שבעים וחד קשיא.

(e) A Tanna taught, *semikhah* and *semikhat zekenim* require three. What is
semikhah and what is *semikhat zekenim*? R. Yochanan said, *mismakh sabei*.
[Fourth-century Amoraim take Yochanan's *mismakh sabei* to be "ordination of
Elders" and continue the discussion asking,] How do we know ordination of
Elders requires three? [Biblical precedent from Moses is rejected, and the
conclusion *koshya'*, i.e., there ought to be biblical evidence but there isn't any,
follows.]

Here too the debate begins with the Simeon-Judah controversy, at which
time our citation is introduced. As in the Palestinian Talmud, so, here, an
independent tannaitic teaching is introduced to prove Simeon's point that three
are required. Here too an independent debate on hermeneutics applied to
sacrifice is turned into another completely separate debate regarding ordination. The connective phrases here, however, are the rhetorical question, "What
is *semikhat zekenim*?" and the answer, a citation from R. Yochanan, which
merely translates the Hebrew *semikhat zekenim* to its Aramaic equivalent,
mismakh sabei.

The only new information here is R. Yochanan's cryptic comment to the effect
that *semikhat zekenim* is *mismakh sabei*. If, indeed, he meant to identify it as
the "ordination of Elders,"[77] we would have evidence of ordination in Palestine in
which three people were required, and we might even argue that *mismakh*
implied laying on of hands. But there is every reason to deny that interpretation.

To begin with, it is unclear why Yochanan, a Palestinian, who always used
minuy for "ordination," would translate *semikhat* as *mismakh* rather than as
minuy, unless, of course, he did not mean ordination at all. It would seem more
logical to assume that he was translating the Hebrew *semikhat zekenim*
directly into its Aramaic equivalent, the spoken vernacular, but had no
intention of altering its biblical meaning relating to the sacrifice of Lev. 4.[77]

The only clear way to deny this alternative interpretation would be to render
mismakh as a verb (to lay hands on), in which case *sabei* would be the direct
object (elders). The only verbal form possible would be the *pe'al* infinitive, but
then we should expect the normal prefix, *lamed*. Indeed, even Levy, who is
quite sure Yochanan meant ordination, is equally positive that we have not a
verb but a construct noun equal to the Hebrew *semikhat*.[78] We have, therefore,
a literal translation of the Hebrew, taken out of context for editorial purposes in
the Babylonian Talmud. There is no way to deduce why Yochanan translated it,
and certainly no reason to believe that fourth-century Babylonians were
correct in identifying Yochanan's intent as ordination.

In sum, taking all five cases together, we find that just as there was never any
laying on of hands, so there was never a ceremony requiring three people.
Semikhah, *semikhut*, and *semikhat* or *semikhot zekenim* all refer to sacrifices.
Editorial style in the Talmuds resulted in later misunderstandings, as people
misinterpreted the connective tissue between two discrete discussions.

One final matter remains before concluding this account. We must demonstrate the consistent use of the term *minuy* for ordination in Palestinian sources, and see what implications that has for us.

4. *Terminology and Conclusion*

All researchers have had to deal with the knotty problem entailed by the fact that even though today ordination is known as *semikhah,* and even though the putative tannaitic proof texts so far discussed often use the verb *smkh* or nominal forms thereof, the normal term for rabbinic appointment—indeed, any appointment, as we shall see—in the Palestinian Talmud is not *smkh* but *mnh* (or the Aramaic equivalent, *mny*). Convinced that there was ordination with the laying on of hands and quorum of three, and recognizing that the proof texts for these contentions always used the word *smkh,* they have had to explain how *mnh* rather than *smkh* can be the only term in the Palestinian Talmud. A way out was seen in the Development Model, according to which it could be assumed that *mnh* replaced *smkh* when the Personal Period ended. Various versions of this theory have been amply documented so far. This view was held even though the Palestinian Talmud itself says that the Babylonian *semikhuta'* is equivalent to the Palestinian *minuy*[79] and nowhere suggests that Palestine once shared this Babylonian nomenclature.

Clearly a more convincing explanation is called for. Rather than postulate a developmental alteration in Palestinian terminology, we may explain the dichotomy as a literary preference that differentiated Palestine from Babylonia.[80] This would explain why the story of Judah ben Baba uses *smkh* while the statement, "Originally everyone used to ordain . . ." used *mnh;* the former is carried only in the Babylonian Talmud, while the latter is only in the Palestinian Talmud. Moreover, whenever the Palestinian Amoraim are cited with *smkh,* the locus of the pericope is the Babli; parallel statements in the Yerushalmi always use *mnh.* P.T. Bik. 3:3, for example, discusses ordination outside the Land of Israel and uses *mnh;* in the Babli the same subject is quoted in the name of a Palestinian (Joshua ben Levi) but with the word *smkh.*[81] More significant still is the amazing fact that the very same *aggadah* is told in the name of R. Eleazer in both Talmuds, but the Babli reads *semikhah* while the Yerushalmi reads *minuy!*[82] Apparently the Babylonians had no compunction against changing the word *minuy* to *semikhah* in their recensions. Thus stories about Palestinian ordination are carried in the Babli with the word *smkh.* We should expect *mnh.* Indeed we probably would have it, but the Babli had edited the stores, changing them regularly to its own preferred terminology. The ordinations of Rabbis Zeira, Ammi, and Assi, for example, all read *smkh;* but that is because they are Babylonian recensions.[83]

A literary model rather than a developmental one allows us to be objective about tannaitic strata. We have seen how the needless focusing on *smkh* in the Mishnah and Tosefta led to false trails in which *semikhah* and *semikhat zekenim* were misinterpreted as "ordination." Having surveyed the root *smkh* in this literature and seen it to mean "sacrifice," "abutment," "adding to," and so on— but not "ordination"—and having discovered that "ordination" was *minuy* in Palestine, let us survey the tannaitic literature again, this time to see how *mnh* is used.

In the Mishnah, the word *mnh* recurs consistently in the sense of "civic appointment."[84] We find appointment of priests, wards for orphans, Temple appointees, the High Priest, and even a king.[85] The Tosefta replicates these instances but adds the appointment of a *Parnas*, a *Yachid*, and a *Talmid Chakham*.[86] We do not find any instance of rabbinic ordination, although considering the *baraita* literature as a whole, we do find an "appointed" Patriarch, first in the case of Hillel, and then with regard to Elazar ben Azariah.[87]

It is clear then that appointment, or *minuy*, was an old custom, going back at least as far as Hillel and the *ta'anit* regulations whence the *Yachid* is known. These regulations precede the Common Era.[88] Temple appointees, too, must at least antecede 70. We have then a rather fluid situation before 70, in which *minuy* described appointees in every area of Jewish life: the court, the Temple, the community, and so on. We do not, however, have rabbis in that time, as the term "Rabbi" comes into being only after 70.

The amazing thing is that we have not a single instance of a man actually receiving the title "Rabbi." In other words, we know that there were rabbis from the year 70 onward, but no source tells us explicitly about them. True, we have Palestinian accounts involving the root *mnh*, and some seem to be about rabbis; but never is the word *mnh* coupled explicitly with the word "rabbi."

It would seem, therefore, that no specific term arose to define rabbinic appointment. Strange as it may seem to us, who single out clerical appointment from all others, ordination in Palestine was subsumed, terminologically at least, along with other civil designations. Rabbis were "ordained" in that they were appointed to specific functions as communal workers; they were part of the civil service of their day. They received their title just as the *Yachid* or the *Parnas* received his. Sometimes, as in the case of Rav (San. 5a), they received no title but certain prerogatives. If there was a liturgical ceremony associated with rabbinic appointment, we do not know anything about it. Most ceremonial claims generally made are based on misinterpretations of the word *smkh*. To be sure, by the late second and early third centuries, rabbinic appointment became a political issue around which the relative strength of the Patriarch and the other rabbis in the scholar class revolved. But the issue here was something akin to modern political patronage. Even in the amoraic sources we have looked at, the rabbi does not emerge as essentially different from the *Parnas*, for example. Both are appointees. Both have their own respective jobs to do.

It happens that the Babli regularly translated Palestinian ordination terminology into its own preferred vocabulary, *semikhah*.[89] Moreover, by the time the Babli was composed, Palestine had successfully asserted its claim to be the sole place where ordination might take place, so that Babylonian discussions of *semikhah* were purely hypothetical anyway. The Babylonian rabbis could freely relate stories of Palestinian ordination and, later, edit them into their Talmud according to the stylistic rules that governed the structure of talmudic literary debate.

Post-talmudic generations made the mistake of taking both Talmuds literally in their respective claims regarding ordination. People came to believe that ordination had really been a unique matter of great mystique practiced solely in

Palestine. More important, they studied the Babli and accepted its unique vocabulary, *semikhah*, as "ordination." It followed then that ordination required three, that there was laying on of hands, and so on.

In modern times, the analogy with Christian ordination has led to a search for something comparable in early Jewish tradition. So scholars have built an elaborate structure of notions presumed to correspond to early ordination ceremonial. There is no evidence to support any of this. Though there may have been some liturgical rite in the tannaitic era, it is now lost to us, buried under the misconceptions and ideological debates of the following centuries.

One must conclude that the question of rabbinic ordination has been poorly put. There is indeed an English word for "ordination," as there is one in other languages influenced by Christian culture. But that word arises out of a Christian context. For ancient Palestinian Jews, there was no corresponding Hebrew or Aramaic word. There was just *minuy*, which meant other things as well.

The real question or questions, then, have yet to be asked. The appropriate task is to isolate titles of Jewish authorities: *Zaken, Parnas*, Rabbi, Rav, *Rabbeinu, Moreinu*, and a whole host of others through Jewish history; and to ask how authority was vested in these people. By operating as we have under the mistaken conception of a metaphysical ordination procedure that began, ended, was almost reinstated, and so on, we remain blind to the multifaceted manifestations of marking Jewish authority throughout the variable circumstances of Jewish history.

The pseudo-task of discovering a hypothetical ordination operative through history must be discarded. The real challenge of investigating authority structures in Jewish societies past and present should now begin.

NOTES

1. W. Bacher, "Zur Geschichte der Ordination," *MGWJ* 38 (1894), p. 122.
2. A. Sidon, "Die Controverse der Synhedrialhäupter," in *Gedenkbuch zur Erinnerung an David Kaufmann*, M. Brann and F. Rosenthal, eds. (Breslau: 1900), p. 360.
3. J. Newman, *Semikhah* (Manchester: 1950), p. 103.
4. See, e.g., Jacob Z. Lauterbach, *Jewish Encyclopedia*, s.v. "Ordination," pp. 428-429.
5. Newman, *Semikhah*, and I.D. Herzog, as cited there, p. 105, n. 3.
6. Bacher, "Geschichte," p. 122.
7. For Isaac ben Reuben al-Bergeloni of Barcelona, see his *Sefer Hashetarot*, S. J. Halberstam, ed. (Berlin: 1898), p. 132. Y. Bornstein ("Mishpat Hasemikhah Vekoroteha," *Hatekufah* 8 [1919], p. 413, n. 2) and Ch. Albeck ("Semikhah and Minui and Beth Din" [Hebrew], *Zion* 8 [1943], p. 86, n. 5) attribute Isaac's error to a faulty recension of the Babylonian Talmud inherited from R. Hananel of Kairuan. For sample *midrashim*, see Dinabourg [Dinur], "The Rescript of Diocletian to Judah in the Year 293, and the Struggle Between the Patriarchate and the Sanhedrin in Palestine" [Hebrew], in *Studies in Memory of Asher Gulak and Samuel Klein*, Simchah Assaf and Gershom Scholem, eds. (Jerusalem: 1942), p. 89.
8. Sidon ("Die Controverse," pp. 356-357) traces the argument to Zacharias Frankel; cf. Bornstein, "Mishpat Hasemikhah," p. 396.
9. M. Hag. 2:3. The debate is for Festival days. For ordinary days, the laying of hands on offerings was never in doubt.
10. T. Hag. 2:8, 2:10. The former is the parallel text, but does not identify the controversy. The latter, however, asks, "Which *semikhah* were they debating?", and then discusses the Hillelite–Shammaite controversy of M. Hag. 2:3. Since the debate of the

zugot (M. Hag. 2:2) ends with Hillel and Shammai, it seems probable that the schools they founded continued this long-standing argument, so that we can view T. Hag. 2:10 as an explanation referring back to T. Hag. 2:8, and thus, interpreting M. Hag. 2:2. On the other hand, this need not be so. If M. Hag. 2:2 is not related to M. Hag. 2:3, T. Hag. 2:10 may have nothing to do with T. Hag. 2:8. Sidon ("Die Controverse," p. 358) takes this latter view, and theorizes that M. Hag. 2:2 is about ordination, and is inserted here because of the Mishnah's tendency to pair subject matters on the basis of word similarity. He further argues that some key words required by the sacrificial context are lacking. Newman (*Semikhah*, p. 11) believes that *semikhah* as ordination existed, so is on Sidon's side of the issue, yet differs in this instance since the "missing" words here are present elsewhere, and the discussion there indicates that sacrifice is being discussed here. Cf. Solomon Zeitlin, "The Semikah Controversy Between the Zugoth," *JQR* 7 (1917), p. 503; he argues that the issue here is neither sacrifice nor ordination, but whether or not one should depend on the authority of the Hakamim.

11. I arrive at this number by counting the listings in Hayyim Yehoshuah Kasovsky, *Thesaurus Mishnae*. The final count varies slightly, depending on such variables as multiple listings.

12. M. Git. 5:4, e.g., discusses minor orphans dependent on a guardian.

13. M. B.B. 2:12, e.g., discusses two farmers with adjoining properties divided by a wall; each may plant a tree as far as the dividing wall.

14. See e.g., M. Tamid 7:3, M. Neg. 14:8, M. Tem. 3:4, and M. Men. 9:7-9.

15. The only possible exception is M. San. 4:4, discussed below. A parallel study of the Tosefta validates these findings, again with one possible exception (carried, however, in several recensions), the issue of *semikhat zekenim*, also discussed below.

16. Chanokh Albeck, *Shishah Sidre Mishnah, Seder Moed* (Israel: 1959), p. 511, n. 2.

17. Saul Lieberman, *Tosefta Kifshutah*, vol. 5 (New York: 1962), p. 1300. See also pp. 1296, 1300-1301, for full analysis.

18. Bacher, "Geschichte," p. 123.

19. "Not everyone who wishes can make himself . . . a *talmid chakham*, unless the *beth din* ordains him" (T. Taan. 1:7). The verb for "ordain" is *mnh* not *smkh*, but we shall see that *mnh* was the normal verb for Palestine. It may be that we should doubt the veracity of this San. 4:4 report at any rate, seeing it as either an anachronistic reading back to earlier times of the structure of Judah I's academy; or simply a stylized account of how the Sanhedrin ought to have worked whether it did so or not. See H. P. Chajes, "Les juges juifs en Palestine de l'an 70 à l'an 500," *REJ* 39 (1899), p. 52. "Il n'existait pas de tribunaux au veritable sense du mot fonctionnant d'une manière permanente."

20. Albeck, *Mishnah, Moed*, p. 511, n. 2; and idem, "Semikhah," p. 85.

21. Sidon, "Die Controverse," p. 363, n. 1. This is another case of the general concept of abutment, mentioned above, n. 13. For example, M. B.B. 1:4 uses *smkh* to describe a wall that abuts (or adjoins) another wall, and thus is part of it. We find similar usage regarding stones that are part of an oven and a *sukkah* that is part of an unclean building (M. Kelim 6:4, M. Ohol. 7:1). So here we have the case of an individual sage who becomes part of the Sanhedrin. The concept of physical abutment is extended to include the notion of personal adjoining.

22. See M. Feinstein, *Hapardes* 17, cited by Newman (*Semikhah*, p. 103), and Albeck ("Semikhah," p. 85), who agree. Among the many problems entailed by the mistaken notion that the laying on of hands was practiced, is the difficulty of accounting for the fact that the Mishnah does not manifestly discuss it. To this, Newman (*Semikhah*, p. 6), following Porath, contends that the Mishnah's author, Judah I, wished to avoid the impression that the laying on of hands was necessary, since he no longer did it. He stopped doing it, we are told, because in the post-Hadrianic era, ordinands were no longer one's personal students (Lauterbach, "Ordination," p. 429); or because Jews wished to avoid what had become a Christian custom (so argue no fewer than six outstanding scholars cited by Newman [*Semikhah*, p. 105], as well as Gaster [Hastings, *Encyclopaedia of Religion and Ethics*, s.v. "Ordination, Jewish," p. 554]; and Lauterbach ["Ordination," p. 429]). The first argument is a weak one, since the absence of personal affection has not prevented the laying on of hands in modern ceremonies. The second argument is dependent on the curious notion that second-century Jews would drop a hallowed custom believed to go back to Moses, rather than cling to it all the more tenaciously, in the face of a Christian claim that it conferred religious authority. Newman is so disturbed by this logic that he cites Herzog, who suggested that Jews discarded the laying on of hands so as to deceive the Romans into thinking that ordination was no longer practiced. All such problems are avoided by holding that Jews simply did not employ the laying on of hands, so there was no such custom to cease or to be recorded in the first place.

23. Cf. Dinabourg [Dinur], "The Rescript of Diocletian," p. 89; Newman, *Semikhah*, p. 109; Aaron Rothkoff, *Encyclopedia Judaica*, s.v. "Semikhah," p. 1140.

24. Salo W. Baron, *A Social and Religious History of the Jews*, 2nd ed. (New York: 1952), vol. 2, p. 201.

25. Gaster, "Ordination," p. 552.

26. For an instance of the latter, see Dinabourg [Dinur], above, n. 23.

27. P.T. San. 19a.

28. B. San. 13b/14a. This story is part of the debate over the number of people required to confer ordination, and is cited to indicate that one rabbi is sufficient. The last sentence is the Gemara's response to the argument, maintaining that the absence of other names in the account should not be taken to imply that Judah acted alone. This sentence (i.e., "Other people . . .") differs from the story itself in that it is probably a later literary stratum. The story is a genuine legend with the probability of some historical validity. But it is used here for the sake of argument, so it prompts an equally argumentative refutation (the last sentence) for which no historical validity should be assumed. Cf. A.Z. 8b.

29. The traditional view championed by Maimonides (d. 1204) is that personal ordination goes back to Moses and Joshua. Lauterbach ("Ordination," p. 248) dates it to the early Second Commonwealth, particularly during the reign of Alexander Jannaeus (104-78 B.C.E.). Newman places it in the time of Gamaliel I (second third of the first century). The ending of this period is also a matter of speculation, Chajes, for example ("Les Juges," p. 42), holding that it continued secretly throughout the persecution period, never ending at all. I argue here that the whole question of chronology is posed erroneously. Both before and after 70, generalized appointments to one thing or another were the norm. Such appointees included but were not limited to people with the title "Rabbi" (though there were no "rabbis" before 70). The only question is the extent to which individuals appointed freely, like feudal nobles; and conversely, how much a centralized patriarchate could limit that freedom. The Personal Period corresponds to decentralization, when societal centrifugal forces still placed local power in the hands of individual rabbis. Since their appointments were equivalent to Jewish autonomous government with, however, no centralized control, Hadrian banned them—stipulating punishment for individual cities, since he recognized the decentralization of Judean society—and substituted martial law for a time. Eventually a strong Patriarch established a controlled system of centralized appointments, and then the Personal Period was over.

30. That is, *befeh*, the system known to R. Zeira, and also (perhaps) to Rav Ashi.

31. See discussion by Dinabourg [Dinur], "The Rescript of Diocletian," p. 91.

32. Cf. Graetz, *Geschichte*, 4th ed., p. 453, n. 25; Chajes, "Les Juges," p. 44; Bacher, "Geschichte," p. 124; Dinabourg [Dinur], "The Rescript of Diocletian," p. 88, n. 6. Bornstein ("Mishpat Hasemikhah," p. 397) also prefers Judah, though Newman (*Semikhah*, p. 19) misunderstands him; Newman's candidate is Simon ben Gamaliel II. Albeck ("Semikhah," p. 89) concludes that there is insufficient evidence to support either case with certainty.

33. For Judah I, see Bornstein, "Mishpat Hasemikhah"; for Gamaliel III, see Chajes, "Les Juges," p. 45, n. 7; for Judah II, see both Graetz, *Geschichte*, vol. 4, pp. 230, 453, and Newman, *Semikhah*, pp. 19-21; for Judah III, see Dinabourg [Dinur], "The Rescript of Diocletian," p. 87. All of these opinions can be traced back much earlier. Weiss and Halevy debated the subject in nineteenth-century literature, and Judah I was first (?) suggested by Rashi in his comment to B.M. 85b, *vela' hava mistaya' milta'*. . . .

34. P.T. Bik. 3:3 = San. 7b, e.g., notes "those appointed by money" (*'ilen demitmenei vekesef*). P.T. San. 7:2 knows of unlearned appointees (*la' gemirei*). The specific patriarch, however, is not named, so these sources are used to support all the above positions. For a collection of such sources, see Bornstein, "Mishpat Hasemikhah," pp. 379-399; and Dinabourg [Dinur], "The Rescript of Diocletian," p. 92.

35. See Alon's balanced treatment, *Mechkarim Betoldot Yisrael*, vol. 2 (Israel: 1958), pp. 15-57; and idem, *Toldot Hayehudim Be'erets Yisrael Bitekufat Hamishnah Vehatalmud* (Israel: 1952), p. 121. Whenever the political controversy began, it reached its peak in the third century during the political chaos and economic devastation that then characterized the Roman empire. See Dinabourg [Dinur], "The Rescript of Diocletian," p. 91.

36. Newman, *Semikhah*, p. 144.

37. Hillel II is the traditional terminal point, cited by Nachmanides (1194-1270) for example. Solomon ibn Adret (1235-1310) concurs regarding the approximate era (see his comment to B.K. 15b). On the other hand, Poznanski (*Die Babylonische Geonim in der Nachgeonischer Zeit*, p. 81), Bornstein ("Mishpat Hasemikhah," p. 413), and Mann (*Texts and Studies*, vol. 2 [Philadelphia: 1931], p. 229) posit much later dates, up to the first

crusade or even as late as Maimonides. There were various attempts to reestablish ordination in Palestine, the most noted being that of Jacob Berab in 1538 (on which, see Newman, *Semikhah,* pp. 158-170; and Meir Beneyahu, "Chidushah shel Hasemikhah Bitsfat," in *Sefer Yovel Leyitschak Baer,* pp. 248-269). Elijah Hakohen is also said to have tried to "renew" *(lechadesh)* ordination in 1083. I doubt that this term implies the reimposition of a practice that had once ceased, however, since the same source uses the same Hebrew verb with the Geonate *(hageonut)* as the object, and we know that the Palestinian Geonate had been reestablished earlier. See the lengthy discussion by Mann, *Texts and Studies,* vol. 2, pp. 229ff.; discussion and sources cited in Newman, *Semikhah,* Chap. 7, and Lawrence A. Hoffman, "Leadership and Tradition in Religious Communities," *Liturgy* 24 (1979): 18-22.

38. San. 5a.
39. For introductory discussions of three levels of authority, see Newman, *Semikhah,* p. 53; Bornstein, "Mishpat Hasemikhah," p. 397; and Epstein, "Ordination et Autorisation," *REJ* 46 (1903), p. 209, where three separate categories—*désigner, ordonner,* and *autoriser*—are postulated.
40. Rothkoff, "Semikhah," p. 1141.
41. Newman, *Semikhah,* pp. 117-121.
42. Lev. R. 2:4.
43. San. 14a; Ket. 17a. The original for "unqualified scholars" is *sarmisin, sarmitin, harmisin, tarmisin.* It has been translated in various ways, ranging from "Those who use foreign words," to "Half-asses and third-asses." See sources in Newman, *Semikhah,* p. 121, n. 3. The "song" for R. Zeira is equally elusive in its individual words, though not its general intent. The last words are *veya'alat khen,* a reference to Pr. 5:19. But the terms for "make-up," "rouge," and "hair-do" are unclear, their precise meaning receiving no scholarly consensus (see Levy, *Wörterbuch* and Jastrow, *Dictionary*).
44. Ket. 17a. We may simply have a wedding song cited transcontextually in a discussion of ordination.
45. Newman, *Semikhah,* p. 121, n. 3.
46. See above, nn. 34-35.
47. Rothkoff, "Semikhah," p. 1142.
48. Proof that Babylonian editing is present here derives from the verb used in the phrase "When they ordained . . ." and in the putative song by the Palestinian people, "Ordain for us." In both cases the verb is *smkh,* which, we shall see, Palestinians did not use for ordination, though Babylonians did.
49. Newman, *Semikhah,* p. 122.
50. San. 7b. The biblical verse is Hab. 2:19. Its use of *yoreh,* the very word used for one of the judicial functions, makes Judah's rebuke forceful. Cf. P.T. Bik. 3:3.
51. Bacher, *Geschichte,* p. 122, based on an interpretation of Ezek. 13:9 by the third-century Amora Eliezer ben Pedat, who takes the word *ketav* (writ) to mean ordination.
52. Newman, *Semikhah,* pp. 126-127. Newman relies on P.T. Bik. 3:3, which he takes to describe a letter given to an ordinand. See also San. 5a = P.T. Hag. 1:8, which he sees also as referring to such a letter.
53. Rothkoff, "Semikhah," p. 1141.
54. Kasovsky, *Thesaurus Mishnae,* vol. 13, p. 1278.
55. See *Aruk Completum,* s.v. Abaye.
56. *Hilkhot Sanhedrin* 4:3 and commentary to M. San. 1:3. For Maimonides' dependence on R. Hananel, see Albeck, "Semikhah," p. 85, n. 1. Hananel's text of San. 13b had R. Yochanan testifying that *semikhat zekenim bisheloshah* meant *mesamekhei sabei* rather than *mismakh sabei* (our text). He read *smkh* as a verb, thus translating it in the sense of "ordaining," and *sabei* as the direct object, i.e., the Elders being ordained. See discussion below.
57. Cf. T. San. 1:1; M. San. 1:3; P.T. San. 19a; B. San. 13b.
58. See, e.g., Newman, *Semikhah,* p. 13.
59. Bornstein, "Mishpat Hasemikhah," p. 396.
60. Newman, *Semikhah,* p. 15. He follows Bacher.
61. Albeck, "Semikhah," p. 89.
62. See above, n. 57.
63. See note 59. Though Bornstein's resolution may not be convincing, the problem remains.
64. Deut. 21:1-9. Cf. *Sifra* ad loc., where three are explicitly assumed.
65. See above, nn. 59-61. Sidon ("Die Controverse," p. 364) concurs.
66. See above, n. 16.
67. See, e.g., Men. 5:7.
68. P.T. San. 19a.

69. See, e.g., Lieberman's text of T. Yeb. 12:10 (*Tosefta Kifshutah*), where a variance in mss. occurs twice in the same passage.

70. Cf. Ex. 29:15, 19, where laying on of hands is called for.

71. Simeon's name appears in parallel texts: P.T. San. 19a; B. San. 13b; T. San. 1:1; M. San. 1:3.

72. See above, n. 71.

73. I would argue that there was a second-century debate between Simeon and Judah. It was purely academic, an exercise in scriptural exegesis, the subject being the Elders' sacrifice of Lev. 4. Simeon's opinion—that it required three—became normative, and was recorded in M. San. 1:3 and T. San. 1:1, where, however, the variant version *semikhut* (or *semikhot*) was used. Since Judah's opinion stated the need for five, not three, and since T. Men. 10:14 discussed five people bringing a sacrifice, this debate was mistakenly inserted there, though it was actually irrelevant in that context. The same debate became the introduction to the amoraic discussion of M. San. 1:3 in both Talmuds.

74. See above, n. 69.

75. For the rest of this text, see above, discussion of Personal Period.

76. Alternatively, the connecting phrase, "In Babylonia . . ." was already appended to the first discussion, either as proof that *semikhut* was not *semikhah*, or independently.

77. Recall R. Hananel's variant text, *mesamekhei sabei*, which would mean "ordaining Elders." But his text is plainly incorrect. See Rabinowitz, *Variae Lectiones in Mischnam et in Talmud [Dikdukei Soferim]*, ad loc. Neither Alfasi nor the fragments known to Teutsch (*Otsar Hageonim Lemassekhet Sanhedrin* [Jerusalem: 1966]) display this variation. I am grateful to my colleague Michael Chernick for suggesting another possibility, however; Yochanan may have meant ordination, and used the normal Palestinian verb *mnh* in his original statement; but the Babylonian editors subsequently altered his parlance to accord with their own linguistic preference. Our discussion in the next section indicates that the Babylonians were not beyond doing so; but we have no evidence, at least in this case, that they did.

78. J. Levy, *Wörterbuch*, vol. 2, p. 171. Jastrow (*Dictionary*) does not discuss our passage.

79. P.T. 19b.

80. This seems to be Albeck's position ("Semikhah," p. 86).

81. Cf. P.T. Bik. 3:3; B. San. 14a.

82. Cf. P.T. San. 1:2, R.H. 2:5, and B. Ket. 112b.

83. San. 14a.

84. Of course it has other meanings too: to count, to be included technically in a sacrificial group, etc. Cf. Kasovsky, *Thesaurus*, s.v. *mnh*.

85. Cf. Men. 4:5, Git. 5:4, Shek. Chap. 5, Hor. 3:3.

86. Cf. T. R.H. 2:3, 2:9; T. B.K. 7:13, T. Taan. 1:7. I have not translated these titles, since literal translations do not explain the roles intended. The *Talmid Chakham* is well known, though his role may not be. The *Yachid* (see M. Taan. 1:4) initiated certain fasting behavior. The *Parnas* was a civic functionary, responsible, among other things, for securing communal tax levies for the Romans. See R. Yochanan's advice to avoid the *boule* (P.T. M.K. 2:3) and discussion by Baron, *History*, vol. II, p. 203. Yochanan's example is amoraic, but may reflect late tannaitic times.

87. T. Pes. 4:14, P.T. Pes. 6:1, B. B.M. 85a, Pes. 66a; P.T. Ber. 4:1, Ber. 27b.

88. Since the mishnaic account still presupposes a *nasi* and an *av bet din* as a standard procedure, we are probably before the time of Gamaliel I. See Solomon Zeitlin, *The Rise and Fall of the Judean State*, vol. 2, p. 302.

89. It did so not only with *minuy*, but also with other terms involving advancement. See Albeck, "Semikhah," p. 87.

FROM WHENCE THE AUTHORITY OF THE RABBI TO COMFORT AND COUNSEL?

HARRY A. ROTH

All of us rabbis are aware, whether we be young or old, novice or veteran, that we, most if not all, have a three-stage thinking process: forethought, thought, and afterthought. Speaking for myself I have found that often, thank God not always, my sermonic afterthoughts are more telling and impacting, more perceptive and more potent, than my forethoughts and thoughts, but usually too late to be of value, at least for the sermon just delivered. A colleague once told me that he (in those days rabbis were always "he") usually delivered three sermons every Friday night—the one he outlined and reviewed in his study ערב שבת, the one he then delivered from the pulpit, and finally the one he delivered in the solitude of his journey home after the service. I share this thought with you because the theme of this paper developed in a somewhat similar pattern. When I first received the invitation from Herman Schaalman to share in this program, I responded with an idea which was readily accepted, then as time passed, while I did not immediately find the time to prepare the paper, I kept having other ideas about the contents of this session. It went from "Who Comforts the Comforter?" to "And Who Counsels the Counselor?" ultimately to rephrasing to fit the session, "From Whence the Authority of the Rabbi to Comfort and Counsel?"

My thoughts were drawn to "comforting and counseling" because when Herman's letter arrived I thought of the many areas of "rabbinic authority," teaching, preaching, and administering: "PR'ing and Good-Willing," pastoring for some and maybe even "plastering," as well as other areas, some inimical, others compatible to Reform Judaism. But I was at that time deeply involved in some tragic congregational situations which were very painful experiences for me personally after a close relationship of almost two decades. And I thought of my pain and my loss and how would I be able to comfort the immediate family members. Even more than that, I wondered why I should have to comfort others when I myself needed comforting. I know, without doubt, that some of these deaths affected me as much, if not more, than some of the immediate family.

We rabbis officiate at life-cycle events which after twenty years of close personal relationship with a congregation cease to be just calendar events and become for the rabbi a personal joy or, as it often happens, a personal tragedy.

All of us encounter untold unpleasant situations, but the longer we remain with a congregation and the closer the bonds are tied, the more difficult it becomes to simply "officiate" at any life-cycle event, and increasingly more so at the time of a tragedy. Those of us who have spent a decade or two and especially more know full well what I mean when I ask, "Who comforts the comforter?" Who comforts the rabbi, who, it seems, is forever destined to be the comforter?

95

Was this always the role of the rabbi? If so, when did it begin? If it is an acquired role, when did it become part of the rabbi's role? In our tradition, the leader, be he prophet, sage, or rabbi, has fulfilled the role of "comforter and counselor." When the matriarch Rebecca was having difficulties with her pregnancy, as we are told in Gen. 25:22: ויתרצצו הבנים בקרבה . . . ותלך לדרש את ד', the verse says and Rashi explains, as we remember, that the term לדרש את ד' really means לבית מדרשו של שם and the Rashbam adds נביאים the prophets of the day.

Perhaps this is the first instance of a Jewish mother (to-be) turning to some form of counseling in search for a solution to a problem. Our colleague Harold Saperstein in his paper speaks of three stages in the development of rabbinic authority, and this instance certainly predates even the first, but the later midrashic explanation of the expected role of the rabbi fits the mold.

Or perhaps we should regard as the first such instance the situation of Hannah חנה (1 Samuel 1:10), who joins her husband אלקנה in Shilo to pour out her heart because of her barrenness, and עלי הכהן, rather than comfort her, at first misunderstanding her plight (1:13), castigates her וַיַחְשְׁבֶהָ עֵלִי לְשִׁכֹּרָה. Realizing his error he attempts to rectify his error and salvage his role by offering some comfort to Hannah (1:17) לְכִי לשלום וֵאלֹהֵי ישראל יִתֵּן אֶת שֵׁלָתֵךְ. He relieves her anxiety and offers her the comforting words she needs to hear.

In the first משנה of פאה and in Talmud Shabbat 127a, as well as in the Baraita and in the prayer from the morning service beginning with אלו דברים שאין להם שעור which lists those acts which have no fixed measure and whose reward is measureless as well, we find "comforting the bereaved." But tradition does not place this responsibility only on the shoulders of the rabbi. נחום אבלים was always the responsibility of all people. In the Book of Job (2:11) we see the tradition in action, when Job's three friends "come to bemoan him and to comfort him," לָבוֹא לָנוּד־לוֹ וּלְנַחֲמוֹ. But in reading Scripture one does find the leader specifically and at times it is the Prophet who comforts his people. Isaiah 40 begins with the words נחמו נחמו עמי. The Prophet like God Himself reaches out to comfort the people (Isaiah 52:9).

In the Newman *Hasidic Anthology* (p. 40, #3), the Medzibozer Rebbe comments "When God calls you 'My People,' *be comforted by this*." And as rabbis, we too speak to עַמִי, "my people."

In Talmud Shabbat 152a a story is told. A man died in the neighborhood of Rabbi Judah. The family had no friends in town, so the rabbi joined them for the seven days of mourning. *And he comforted the mourners* (Montefiore & Loewe, *Rabbinic Anthology*, p. 279).

Harold Saperstein proposes in the paper he delivered that there were three periods in the development of "rabbinic authority," each different in many respects, but throughout all these periods, the leaders attained real authority as the result of scholarly attainments. "The authority of the rabbi historically has not inhered in his office but has emerged from his qualifications." As he says, "*Semicha* did not *confer* authority. It was *evidence* of authority." But because mastery of the law was achieved by the rabbi, the right authority was his. In the second period of which Harold speaks, i.e., Middle Ages and the Renaissance, the same attitudes still prevailed, even if with considerable change.

Only in the third stage, the Emergence of the Modern Rabbi, because Jewish life is no longer all-embracing, has there been appreciable change. "Old standards of authority are no longer applicable." In this new world where social patterns and Christian influence have changed our way of life and have affected our religious ways as well, we respond to and fill a new role. Often, perhaps too often, the authority of the rabbi is the result of voluntary acceptance. And now, to be accepted, qualifications may be more essential than in earlier generations.

It seems rather evident that the authority of the rabbi, in some areas such as counseling and comforting, is today by virtue of the people's acceptance. The rabbi who is recognized for his skills in helping people because of his training and practice becomes the leader because of the people's choice. Not because he is the rabbi necessarily, but rather because he is the expert. Some of our rabbinic colleagues are so certain that the role of comforting and counseling can only be fulfilled by those skilled in this discipline, and exclusively dedicated to it, that they have chosen to leave the rabbinate and devote full time and effort to counseling and comforting. Is this not indicative that for some, not the ordained rabbi but the specially trained are destined to help relieve the anxieties and problems which plague so many of our people?

Having said what I have, I must now revert to the thoughts which have gone through my mind from the moment I began to think about this problem. That is, I continue to believe that comfort we must, in our role as rabbis, *because we are rabbis*. The youngest of our colleagues, the most fledgling of all, may very well find on the very first morning of his or her rabbinic pulpit, the need to comfort the bereaved. The mourning family will expect the rabbi to respond to that need, not because of years of training and the accumulation of expertise, but simply because at that moment of need for comfort, understanding is expected from the rabbi. I would maintain that this role has been the rabbi's from time immemorial.

I am not particularly pleased with this obligation. Often I am tempted to question, as did Moses (Ex. 3:11) מִי אָנֹכִי כִּי אֵלֵךְ, or to shrink back and question, as did Jeremiah (1:6) הִנֵּה לֹא יָדַעְתִּי דַּבֵּר כִּי נַעַר אָנֹכִי, or attempt to flee the situation, as did Jonah, whose actions spoke louder than his words.

I believe that as a rabbi I have no choice but to fulfill many obligations, one of which is to comfort. That has been, as I understand it, our tradition.

But at the very same time, I follow good Jewish tradition when I ask: Why me?

The Sages taught that God Himself comforted His people. "The loving deeds on which the rabbis lay most stress—comforting the mourners, visiting the sick, clothing the naked, burying the dead, joining in the rejoicing of the bride and bridegroom—were all said to be deeds which, in the biblical story, had been done by God Himself. The truest rule or principle for human goodness was the Imitation of God" (Montefiore & Loewe, *Rabbinic Anthology*, p. 279).

And if we are to emulate God to attain this highest rung of life, then by all means מדת בשר ודם must be the same as מדת הקב"ה.

And if Isaiah 52:9 and 6:13 can speak of God comforting His people, and if Zechariah can say (1:17): וְנִחַם ד' עוֹד אֶת צִיוֹן "the Lord shall yet comfort Zion," then surely we, inheritors of the tradition, be it prophetic or talmudic, medieval or modern, have *not* only the right to comfort, by virtue of our training and expertise, but the *obligation* to comfort our people, by virtue of the tradition which is ours.

Be this task difficult, or even *terribly* difficult for reasons of personal attachment and intimate involvement over many years, yet the duty remains ours to remember the words of Isaiah 52:9 כִּי נִחַם ד' עַמּוֹ "God comforts His people." And 66:13 כֵּן אָנֹכִי אֲנַחֶמְכֶם . . . so will I comfort you."

A KIND WORD FOR THE "SERMON"

DAVID POLISH

The spoken religious word, uttered by the rabbi, still serves a purpose in the synagogue. Over the years, it has steadily lost importance. It has been replaced by a variety of substitutes—visiting speakers, media events, questions from the congregation. When the rabbi does speak, he often betrays either his disdain or his fear of the carefully prepared word by preparing superficially or hardly at all. He justifies this by deprecating the importance and the influence of the spoken word. So why bother? But are the substitutes for the word any more important or persuasive?

Yet there are serious reasons for being wary of the spoken word. After an age during which demagogues and evil men destroyed a world through the words of their mouths, the destructive power of oratory can have a deterring effect. It is not that the word carries too little weight, but too much force. So may some of its detractors reason. Some of the world's most compelling orators have given it over to death. Nahum Goldmann writes with contempt of oratory because it is a form of mass hypnotism by which the orator can seduce his audiences. Hence, I prefer "spoken word" to "oratory." I also prefer *dvar Torah* to "sermon." That latter term implies a stylized, formal body of rhetoric that for vast audiences is dated in addition to being monitory and hortatory. It also suggests a style and delivery reminiscent of the Christian pulpit. I had a homiletics professor who insisted that homiletics was "the science of writing and delivering sermons." Science! Not skill, nor art, which are also inadequate descriptions. But science? Why not technology? Hence my preference for *dvar Torah*, evoking a presentation rooted in our religious literature, past and present, and addressing an audience face to face, rather than from above. Yet these preferences in no way invalidate my concern for the spoken word, informed with Jewish content, concern, and direction.

There are times when, venturing into a synagogue where the word is not spoken, I feel deprived. Even the grandeur of the authentic Jewish liturgy is impaired if the spoken word is not carefully studied and then presented. By "study" I mean a lifetime of devotion to Torah so that its instruction is available to us when we require it. During the Syrian missile crisis, I walked into a Kurdish synagogue in Jerusalem on a Shabbat morning when war with Syria appeared imminent. There was palpable anxiety everywhere. Yet, despite the fervor of the *tefillot*, not a word was said about what agitated everyone—not a word of hope, comfort, or strength. The absence of the word was painful. On another Shabbat, I sat in the Great Synagogue of Tel Aviv where about fifty old Jews, a father, and his Bar Mitzvah son davened. During *kriat ha-Torah* a group of about thirty strangers, wearing red and white tourists' hats, entered the synagogue. There was agitated conversation and head-turning among the worshippers, and the epithet "goyim" flashed across the aisles. One Jew did go over to talk with the visitors. When the *tefillot* had ended, and the congregation was dispersing, I saw the visitors clustered at the entrance. Each carried an identification tag indicating that he or she was a member of a Danish tour. I sought out the one person in the group who spoke English and conveyed my gratitude, as a Jew and a rabbi, for the Danish people's compassionate treatment of the Jews during World War II. Why was there no discourse from the pulpit about Danish heroism, about *chassside umot ha-olam*, about the need to remember not only Amalek but anti-Amalek? There was a spiritual void in that community that Shabbat morning because it was not deemed fit to express an appropriate word of Torah.

In considering the function of the spoken word, style is irrelevant. Styles change in speaking as they do in literature, in music, in painting—and not always for the better. But despite discontent with prevalent and changing styles, one does not dispense with or minimize the value of literature and the arts. Unquestionably, many forms of expression now compete not only with the word from the pulpit but with the word in the newspaper, the magazine, and the book. They are here to stay, but for great numbers of people, cable TV will become an accessory, not a replacement for the book. Nor can other devices—pop or mechanized—replace the value and even the need by many for the word spoken to a congregation during services. The proliferating media will undoubtedly challenge the rabbi to do his best or else be deserted, but the need will not disappear. Congregations do turn out, week in week out, to hear rabbis. They do not turn out in throngs, but the aggregate of worshippers and listeners in any large community on a Shabbat is not to be discounted. Again and again, congregations make it known, in judging a rabbi or in seeking a rabbi, that what he has to say is important to them.

It is argued, unconvincingly, that there are more effective devices for reaching hearts and minds than through the pulpit. Adult education? The importance of Torah study cannot be overestimated, even if it penetrates only a single soul. But if we evaluate the respective merits of the pulpit and the classroom in terms of numbers, the pulpit, with all of its deficiencies, is still preeminent. Let us foster Torah study *lishmah* but not as an answer to a problematic pulpit. In such a context, the argument for Torah does not stand up. Besides, most of my Torah students were also at services on Shabbat, and most of them came to Torah out of the stimulus generated on Shabbat. What, as I see it, is the basic difference between the pulpit and the classroom? The goal of one is *Torah l' maaseh*, the other is *Torah lishmah*. *Torah l'maaseh* means not only the impulse toward *tikun olam* but also toward *tikum atzmi*, toward *tshuvah*. *Torah lishmah* is a form of *tikun atzmi*. Each road is different, requiring its own special vehicle. Neither road may be bypassed. Each should instruct, each should motivate, but the primary emphases differ markedly. I never left a Sunday morning sermon by Abba Hillel Silver without wanting to respond by some act, and I never left a lecture by Gershom Scholem at the Hebrew University without wanting to learn more.

Are pastoral work, counseling, person-to-person relationships, more effective than "preaching"? Of course, they are an indispensable part of the rabbi's task, but they serve a different set of functions. There is a substantive difference between serving the individual and leading the community. The pulpit is where leadership can and should be exercised. The rabbi's study is where support is offered. A rabbi can counsel more effectively in interpersonal encounter. He can awaken the collective will to live Jewishly from the pulpit. I don't believe that members of my congregation would have accompanied me to Selma, Alabama, and joined the civil rights cause without it. I don't believe that our *Chug* (Chavura) program would have begun auspiciously and flourished, or that a significant number of people would have begun to live Jewishly observant lives without it. I say this with full awareness that we can make only the most modest claims for success in any of our endeavors. But in a society where measurement of anything spiritual against the standards of prevalent paganism is bound to be disheartening, we have no choice but to persevere. What standing, after all, does Sir George Szolti have today against Reggie Jackson? But the comparison in standings *tomorrow* is another matter.

Is it possible that the "sermon" has fallen on difficult times because the task of the rabbi has expanded. He perceives the increasing responsibilities to be so vast that congregations will be forgiving if the "sermon" is neglected in favor of the hospital visit. If this is in fact the case, then the rabbinate is in trouble, and so are congregations. Then congregations and rabbis, as they become more service-oriented, are in the process of losing much of their collective Jewish motivation. They begin to take on the appearance of old New England churches where each family sat in its own walled-in cubicle during worship. If a rabbi must make choices between pastoral and pulpit leadership tasks, then the American synagogue must seek ways of giving him relief. One way is the restoration of pastoral work to the people. This is a precious *mitzvah* which has been relegated to the rabbi. Not that he should be absolved of it, but that it should be shared with him. Several years ago, my congregation established an *Ozrim* program in which a group of about twenty men and women undertook and were trained for intervention in personal and family crisis, helping the sick and the bereaved, visiting shut-ins, in coordination with the rabbi. (The impulse for this was generated from the pulpit.) But other tasks, such as "preaching," belong to the rabbi alone, unless there are others in the congregation with equivalent credentials. Efforts at "filling in" for rabbis when they are away by journalists, political scientists, and other highly qualified people in their fields are the best proof, confirmed by discerning laymen, that the rabbi fulfills a unique role in the pulpit. The most trying task in a congregation can be the preparation of a *dvar Torah*. Is this why some Rabbis evade the task or put it down as obsolete or unworthy of their best efforts? But a *dvar Torah* can also be most rewarding and, to be honest, ego-gratifying. But it is more than that. Where, over the years, a rabbi presents *divrei Torah* that make up a coherent view of Judaism and of life, he may see his congregation moving, not randomly through indecision or convulsively through frenetic projects, but teleologically. Where else can a rabbi declare his credo, where else can he call upon his people to take a stand of mind or conscience or action? Where else can the rabbi most vigorously assert one dimension of his total role which must not be eradicated, leadership?

Retraining for the pulpit is clearly required. A new approach to preparing students for the pulpit, aimed at raising their esteem of it, is called for. But indispensable to all this is a commitment to continuous Jewish study, old and new, without which the spoken word rings hollow.

Concluding his *Die gottesdienstlichen Vorträge der Juden historisch entwik- kelt* Zunz writes: "Whether the speaker is known as preacher or rabbi, teacher or orator, [it matters not] as long as he will know how to find the word of God in Scripture or Aggadah, and will know how to extract gold from matters old and new, to reveal in the present the true destiny, and to choose the right expression for penetrating the heart. Then the spirit of God will return to dwell in your sacred places, O daughter of Zion, and His voice will again be heard in speech that arouses to deeds, in speech full of enthusiasm which will establish institutions for Israel. The spark that will be struck will not again be extinguished; persecution will only quicken it to a glowing flame . . ."

RABBINIC AUTHORITY VIS À VIS CHRISTIANITY
AN OUTLINE

MICHAEL J. COOK

The following outline was prepared in conjunction with texts read as part of a conference program session.

Ancient Times

I. Early Attempts to Contrast the AUTHORITY OF JESUS—with the AUTHORITY OF THE RABBIS
    A. *Traditions Concerning Jesus' Authoritative Manner:*
        1. Mt. 21:23;
        2. Mk. 1:21–28;
        3. Mk. 6:2–3.
    B. *Designations of Jesus as a "Rabbi"—What Is Their Significance?*
        1. Jn. 1:47–49;
        2. Jn. 3:1–2;
        3. Jn. 1:38;
        4. Jn. 20:15–16.
    C. *Assessing the Authority of the Rabbi—Early Christian Disparagements:*
        1. Mt. 23:1ff.;
        2. Mt. 23:27–28;
        3. Justin Martyr's *Dialogue with Trypho*—Sections 141; 38; 112.
    D. *A Medieval Perspective:*
    Disputation of Barcelona (1263).
    E. *Summary.*

II. Early Impingements of Rabbinic Authority on Christianity
    A. *Scriptural Exegesis:*
        1. Challenging the authority of the Septuagint (*Dialogue* 71; 68).
        2. Interpreting the meaning of Scriptural passages
        (*Dialogue*, introductory sections; 62; 43).
        3. Rabbinic prohibitions—
        Discourse with Christians (*Dialogue* 38).
        Acceptance of Gospels (T. Shabbat 13:5; T. Yadaim 2:13).
    B. *Synagogue Observance:*
        1. Concerning the Christian Sabbath (Taanith 27b).
        2. Liturgical considerations (Berachoth 28b-29a; *Dialogue* 137; P. Berachoth I.8; 3c).

C. *Christian Involvement in Other Activities:*
1. Healing (T. Hullin 2:22–23).
2. Missionizing (Mt. 28:18–20; Mt. 23:15; *Dialogue* 108).
D. *Summary.*

Modern Times

The following texts were presented and discussed in relation to their place in the above outline:

COMPANION TEXTS

ANCIENT TIMES

I. Early Attempts to Contrast the Authority of Jesus—with the Authority of the Rabbis
A. *Traditions Concerning Jesus' Authoritative Manner:*
1. Matthew 21:23—And when he entered the temple, the chief priests and the elders of the people came up to him as he was teaching, and said, *"By what authority are you doing these things, and who gave you this authority?"*
2. Mark 1:21–28—And they went into Capernaum; and immediately on the sabbath he entered the synagogue and taught. And they were astonished at his teaching, *for he taught them as one who had authority,* and not as the scribes. And immediately there was in their synagogue a man with an unclean spirit; and he cried out, "What have you to do with us, Jesus of Nazareth? Have you come to destroy us? I know who you are, the Holy One of God."

   But Jesus rebuked him, saying, "Be silent, and come out of him!" And the unclean spirit, convulsing him and crying with a loud voice, came out of him. And they were all amazed, so that they questioned among themselves, saying, "What is this? A new teaching! *With authority* he commands even the unclean spirits, and they obey him."
3. Mark 6:2–3—And on the sabbath he began to teach in the synagogue; and many who heard him were astonished, saying, *"Where did this man get all this? What is the wisdom given to him?* Is not this the carpenter, the son of Mary and brother of James and Joses and Judas and Simon, and are not his sisters here with us?" And they took offense at him.
B. *Designations of Jesus as a "Rabbi"—What Is Their Significance?*
1. John 1:47–49—Jesus saw Nathanael coming to him, and said of him, "Behold, an Israelite indeed, in whom is no guile!" Nathanael

said to him, "How do you know me?" Jesus answered him, "Before
Philip called you, when you were under the fig tree, I saw you."
Nathanael answered him, "*Rabbi*, you are the Son of God! You are
the King of Israel!"

2. John 3:1–2—Now there was a man of the Pharisees, named
   Nicodemus, a ruler of the Jews. This man came to Jesus by night
   and said to him, "*Rabbi, we know that you are a teacher* come from
   God; for no one can do these signs that you do, unless God is with
   him."

3. John 1:38—Jesus turned, and saw them following, and said to
   them, "What do you seek?" And they said to him, "*Rabbi*" *(which
   means Teacher)*, "where are you staying?"

4. John 20:15–16—Jesus said to her, "Woman, why are you weeping?
   Whom do you seek?" Supposing him to be the gardener, she said to
   him, "Sir, if you have carried him away, tell me where you have
   laid him, and I will take him away." Jesus said to her, "Mary." She
   turned and said to him in Hebrew, "*Rabboni!*" *(which means
   Teacher)*.

C. *Assessing the Authority of the Rabbi—Early Christian Disparage-
   ments:*

   1. Matthew 23:1ff.—Then said Jesus to the crowds and to his
      disciples, "*The scribes and the Pharisees sit on Moses' seat; so
      practice and observe whatever they tell you, but not what they do;
      for they preach but do not practice. . . .* They do all their deeds to
      be seen by men; for they make their phylacteries broad and their
      fringes long, and they love the place of honor at feasts and the best
      seats in the synagogues, and salutations in the market places, *and
      being called rabbi by men.*

      But you are not to be called rabbi, for you have one teacher, and
      you are all brethren. And call no man your father on earth, for you
      have one Father, who is in heaven. Neither be called masters, for
      you have one master, the Christ.

      He who is greatest among you shall be your servant; whoever
      exalts himself will be humbled, and whoever humbles himself will
      be exalted.

   2. Matthew 23:27–28—" *. . . Woe to you, scribes and Pharisees,
      hypocrites!* for you are like whitewashed tombs, which outwardly
      appear beautiful, but within they are full of dead men's bones and
      all uncleanness. So you also outwardly appear righteous to men,
      but within you are full of hypocrisy and iniquity. . . ."

   3. Justin Martyr's *Dialogue with Trypho*—" . . . I exhort you . . . to
      be careful to prefer the Christ of Almighty God *to your teachers.*"
      (Section 141)

      Justin Martyr's *Dialogue with Trypho*—" . . . be not troubled, but
      rather continue more diligent hearers and enquirers, disregard-

ing *the tradition of your teachers, who are* convicted by the spirit of prophecy of being *unable to comprehend what God has spoken, and rather preferring to teach their own doctrines. . . .*" (Section 38)

Justin Martyr's *Dialogue with Trypho*—"But you . . . explain these facts in a low manner, . . . and do not search out the force of what is recorded. . . . Shall the [brazen] serpent then . . . be conceived to have . . . saved the people? *And shall we receive such things in the foolish manner in which your teachers lay them down, and not as types?* And shall we not refer the sign to the image of Jesus who was crucified, since also Moses by stretching out his hands together with him who was surnamed Jesus, caused your nation to have the victory? . . . But if *your teachers* only explain to you why female camels are not mentioned in this or that passage, or what kind of animals they are which are called female camels, and why so many measures of fine flour, and so many of oil, are used in the offerings, and that in a low and grovelling manner, but never venture to speak of or explain such things as are of consequence and worthy of investigation, *or even charge you never at all to give ear to us who do explain them, nor to hold any communication with us,* will they not deserve what our Lord Jesus Christ said to them, 'Whited sepulchres, which appear beautiful outward, and are within full of dead men's bones; ye pay tithe of mint, ye swallow a camel, ye blind guides'?

"Unless therefore you despise the doctrines *of those who exalt themselves, and seek to be called Rabbi, Rabbi,* and apply with such constancy and understanding to the writings of the Prophets, that you would suffer at the hands of your nation the same things as the Prophets themselves suffered, you will be unable to derive any benefit whatever from the Prophetic writings." (Section 112)

D. *A Medieval Perspective:*

Disputation of Barcelona (1263)—"Fra Paulo then began: 'This is what we have in scripture, in Genesis 49:10: "The sceptre shall not depart from Judah . . . until Shiloh come." It is the Messiah who is here meant, and the prophet asserts that Judah will always possess power until the Messiah who proceeds from him shall come. That being so, today when you Jews have no longer any sceptre or ruler's staff [or lawgiver], it follows that the Messiah, who is of the seed of Judah and whose is the rulership, has already come.'

"*. . . At the present time you Jews have no longer ordination of scholars which was known to the Talmud.* So even that ruling power has now come to an end. *And today there is no one among you fit to be called Rabbi.'* . . ."

II. Early Impingements of Rabbinic Authority on Christianity
  A. *Scriptural Exegesis:*
    1. Challenging the authority of the Septuagint—
      a. Justin Martyr's *Dialogue with Trypho*—"But I differ from *your teachers, who do not allow that the translation of the seventy Elders in the time of Ptolemy, the king of Egypt, was well done, and endeavor to make a translation themselves. . . .*" (Section 71)
      b. Justin Martyr's *Dialogue with Trypho*—". . . shall I not make you ashamed of believing *your teachers . . . who presume to affirm that the translation which your seventy elders made in the time of Ptolemy the king of Egypt is in some respects untrue?*" (Section 68)
    2. Interpreting the meaning of Scriptural passages—
      a. Justin Martyr's *Dialogue with Trypho*—" . . . May it be forgiven you; for . . . you follow *your teachers, who understand not the Scriptures, and utter at random whatever comes into your mind. . . .* (Introductory Sections)
      b. Justin Martyr's *Dialogue with Trypho*—" . . . 'Let us make man in Our Image, and after Our likeness. . . .' But that you may not pervert the meaning of these words, by urging *what your teachers tell you.* that God either said, 'Let Us make,' to Himself . . . or to the elements. . . ." (Section 62)
      c. Justin Martyr's *Dialogue with Trypho*—"Now that no one in the generation of Abraham according to the flesh was ever born, or said to have been born, of a virgin, except this our Christ, is plain to all; but, since you and *your teachers* presume to assert that it is not said in Isaiah, 'Behold a virgin shall conceive,' but, 'Behold a young woman shall conceive, and bear a son,' and explain the prophecy [in connection with] . . . Hezekiah your king, I will endeavor briefly to interpret it against this view, and to show that it is spoken of Him Whom we confess to be Christ." (Section 43)
    3. Rabbinic prohibitions—
      a. Discourse with Christians:
        Justin Martyr's *Dialogue with Trypho*—"To this Trypho replied, 'It would be well for us, Sir, *to obey our teachers, who direct us to give ear to none of your sect, and not to hold any communication with you on these subjects*, for you have spoken many blasphemies, endeavouring to persuade us that . . . He was made man, was crucified, and went up into Heaven, and will again return to the earth, and is to be worshipped' " (Section 38)
      b. Acceptance of Gospels
        1) T. Shabbat 13:5—"The *Gilyonim* and books of the Minim they do not save, but these are burnt in their place, they and

their 'memorials.' . . . R. Tarphon said, ' . . . If the pursuer were pursuing after me, I would enter into a house of idolatry, but I would not enter into their houses. For the idolaters do not acknowledge Him and speak falsely concerning Him; but these [the Minim] do acknowledge Him and speak falsely concerning Him.' . . . R. Ishmael said, 'Whereas, in order to make peace between a man and his wife, God says, "Let my name which is written in holiness be blotted out in water" [Numbers 5:23], how much more the books of the Minim, which put enmity and jealousy and strife between Israel and their Father who is in Heaven, should be blotted out, and their memorials too.' "

2) T. Yadaim 2:13—"The *Gilyonim* and the books of the Minim do not render the hands unclean.

"The books of Ben Sira and all books which have been written from that time onward do not render the hands unclean."

B. *Synagogue Observance:*

1. Concerning the Christian Sabbath—
Tannith 27b—" . . . Why did they not fast on the day after the Sabbath? R. Johanan says, 'Because of the *Nazarenes.*' "

2. Liturgical considerations—

a. Berachoth 28b-29a—"Our rabbis teach: 'Simeon the cotton-seller arranged the Eighteen Benedictions in the presence of Rabban Gamaliel, according to their order, in Yabneh. Rabban Gamaliel said to the Sages, "Is there anyone who knows how to compose a *'Benediction' of the Minim?*" Samuel the Small stood up and composed it. . . .' "

b. Justin Martyr's *Dialogue with Trypho*—
"Agree with us then, and do not scoff at the Son of God, nor persuaded by *your teachers the Pharisees*, ever heap insults on the King of Israel, as *the rulers of your synagogues teach you to do after your prayers.* . . ." (Section 137)

c. P. Berachoth I, 8; 3c—"R. Mathnah and R. Samuel bar Nahman both say: 'It would be in order to read the Ten Commandments every day. Why do we not read them? Because of *the claim of the Minim;* that they should not say, "These alone were given to Moses on Sinai." ' "

C. *Christian Involvement in Other Activities:*

1. Healing—
T. Hullin 2:22-23 (cf. P. Shabbath 14d; P. Abodah Zarah 40d-41a; Abodah Zarah 27b)—"It happened with R. Eleazar b. Damah, whom a serpent bit, that Jacob, a man of Kefar Soma, came to *heal him in the name of Yeshua ben Pantera; but R. Ishmael did not let him.*

"He said, 'You are *not permitted*, Ben Damah.'

"He answered, 'I will bring you proof *that he may heal me.*'

"But he had no opportunity to bring proof, for he died. [Whereupon] R. Ishmael said, 'Happy art thou, Ben Damah, for you have gone in peace and you have not broken down the fence of the Sages; since everyone who breaks down *the fence of the Sages*, to him punishment will ultimately come, as it is in Scripture:

"Whoso breaketh through a fence, a serpent shall bite him." ' "

2. Missionizing—

    a. Matthew 28:18–20—And Jesus came and said to him, "All authority in heaven and on earth has been given to me. Go therefore and *make disciples of all nations* [gentiles?], baptizing them in the name of the Father and of the Son and of the Holy Spirit, teaching them to observe all that I have commanded you; and lo, I am with you always, to the close of the age."

    b. Matthew 23:15—" . . . Woe to you, scribes and Pharisees, hypocrites! for you traverse sea and land *to make a single proselyte,* and when *he becomes a proselyte,* you make him twice as much a child of hell [Gehenna] as yourselves. . . ."

    c. Justin Martyr's *Dialogue with Trypho*—" . . . yet not only did you not repent when you learnt that He had risen from the dead, but, as I said, *you commissioned chosen men,* and sent them throughout the whole world to declare that 'an atheistical and lawless heresy has been raised by one Jesus, a deceiver from Galilee, whom we crucified, but His disciples stole Him by night from the tomb in which he was laid, when unnailed from the cross, and now deceive mankind, saying that He has risen from the dead, and gone up into heaven.' . . . And besides all this, even now that your city is taken and your land laid waste, you do not repent, but even presume to curse Him and all who believe in Him. . . ." (Section 108)

SUGGESTED READING LIST

BOOKS

Gelber, Sholome Michael: *The Failure of the American Rabbi: A Program for the Revitalization of the Rabbinate in America* (New York: Twayne, 1961).

Gottschalk, Alfred: *Your Future as a Rabbi: A Calling that Counts* (New York: Richard Rosen Press, 1967).

Gruenewald, Max: *The Modern Rabbi*, Leo Baeck Institute Yearbook, Vol. II.

Katz, Robert C.: *The Role of the Rabbi in Human Relations: Selected Readings* (Cincinnati: Hebrew Union College–Jewish Institute of Religion, Dept. of Human Relations, 1957).

———: *Changing Self-Concepts of Reform Rabbis* (Cincinnati: Hebrew Union College–Jewish Institute of Religion, Dept. of Human Relations, 1975).

Lenn, Theodore I., et al.: *Rabbi and Synagogue in Reform Judaism* (New York: Central Conference of American Rabbis, 1972).

Litvin, Baruch: *Jewish Identity: Modern Responsa and Opinions* (New York: Feldheim, 1965).

Polner, Murray: *Rabbi: The American Experience* (New York: Holt, Rinehart and Winston, 1977).

ARTICLES IN THE *CCAR YEARBOOK*

Bloom, Jack: "The Rabbi's Family" (1976), pp. 105–114.

Brooks, Sidney H.; Jacobson, David; Levenson, Joseph; and Fierman, Floyd S.: "An Evaluation of Institutes on Judaism (Symposium): The Rabbi and the Non-Jewish Community; What Shall a Rabbi Say to a Christian Congregation?; The Reform Synagogue as Jewish Spokesman; Recorder's Report" (1958), pp. 181–187.

CCAR Committee on Conditions in the Rabbinate: "Report" (1936), pp. 86–88.

CCAR Committee on Justice and Peace: "The Rabbi and the Political Process," in "Report" (1964), pp. 85–86.

CCAR Committee on Mediation and Ethics: "Code of Ethics Between Rabbi and Rabbi," in "Report" (1964), pp. 88–89.

CCAR Committee on Rabbinical Status: "Report" (1965), pp. 89–92.

———: "Report" (1966), p. 75.

———: "Report" (1967), p. 75–77.

———: "Report" (1968), p. 107–109.

———: "Suggestions for Procedure in Rabbinical-Congregational Relationship (Revised)," in "Report" (1969), pp. 150–158.

CCAR Committee on Resolutions: "Resolution on the Ordination of Women to the Rabbinate" (1922), p. 51.

———: "Resolution on Rabbinic-Congregational Relations" (1931), pp. 163–164.

———: "Resolution on Relationship of a Single Rabbi and His Colleagues Outside His Community" (1965), p. 120.

———: "Resolution on the Position of the Rabbinate" (1966), pp. 100–102.

CCAR Committee on the Survey of Rabbinical Activities: "Report" (1930), pp. 109–111.

Freehof, Solomon B., and Silver, Abba Hillel: "The American Rabbinate in Our Lifetime: A Symposium" (1963), pp. 159–172.

Glazer, Nathan: "The Function of the Rabbi" (1967), pp. 130–156.

Goldman, Robert P.: "Cooperation Between the Rabbi and the Layman" (1938), pp. 277–279.

Goldstein, Sidney I.: "The Rabbi in His Role as Pastor" (1957), pp. 124–126.

Goodman, Alfred: "The Inner Life of the Rabbi" (1980), pp. 150–153.

Isserman, Ferdinand, M.: "The Rabbi and the Community" (1953), pp. 341–347.

Katz, Robert: "The Modern Rabbi" (1980), pp. 123–127.

Kornfeld, Joseph S.: "The Changing Functions of the Rabbinate" (1925), pp. 311–325.

Lauterbach, Jacob B.: "Responsum on the Question, 'Is It True That a First Opinion Is Legally and Ethically Binding on the One Who Asks a Rabbinic Authority?' " (1932), pp. 83–84.

Lenn, Theodore I.: "Research Study on Reform Judaism" (1972), pp. 116–144.

Levine, Raphael H.; Sanders, Ira C.; Wice, David H.; and Fine, Hillel A.: "Out of My Experience (Seminar): Too Soon Old—Too Late Smart; Gleanings from the Vineyard; Mementoes of a Pastoral Ministry; Recorder's Report" (1960), pp. 127–134.

Lieberman, Morris; Minda, Albert G.; Emanuel, Nathan; and Goldburg, Robert E.: "A Rabbi's Relationship to Colleagues and the Temple Staff (Symposium): Relationships Between Rabbis in the Same Congregation; A Rabbi's Relationship to Colleagues in the Same Community; The Lay Professional Staff and the Rabbi; Recorder's Report" (1958), pp. 166–173.

Lieberman, Morris: "The Role and Functions of the Modern Rabbi" (1969), pp. 211–234.

Minda, Albert G.: in "The President's Message" (1962), pp. 13–15.

Philipson, David; Kohler, K.; Margolis, Max; Deutsch, G.; and Stolz, Joseph: "Report of the Committee on the Relation between Rabbi and Congregation" (1903), pp. 46–50.

Plaut, W. Gunther: "The People of the Tent" (1962), pp. 184–188.

Polish, Daniel: "Report of the Committee on Rabbinic Training" (1968), pp. 95–96.

———: "The Modern Rabbi" (1980), pp. 127–143.

Prinz, Deborah: "Today's Rabbinate: The Personal Equation" (1980), pp. 148–150.

Reichert, Victor E.; Kramer, Marcus; and Einhorn, Ephraim: "The Inner Life of the Rabbi (Symposium): The Intellectual; The Devotional Life of the Rabbi; Recorder's Report" (1959), pp. 177–182.

Sack, Eugene J.: "The Rabbi as Teen-Age Counselor" (1958), p. 160.

Schulman, Samuel: "A Conference Sermon: The Function of the Rabbi in His Relation to His People (Text: *Numbers* xxiii, 9)" (1906), pp. 205–221.

Sigel, Louis J.: "The Modern Rabbi" (1980), pp. 119–123.

Soloff, Rav, and Schulweis, Harold: "Changing Models of the Synagogue and of the Rabbi's Role" (1975), pp. 131–143.

Stern, David: "Sorry, Wrong Title: The Modern Rabbinate Minus the Equation" (1980), pp. 145–148.

Stolz, Joseph: "The Central Conference, a Professional Body," in "President's Message" (1906), pp. 236–238.

Sundheim, Adrianne: "The Personal Equation of a Rabbi's Life" (1980), pp. 153–157.

Waller, Herbert S.: "Changing Patterns of the Rabbi's Function" (1955), pp. 119–120.

Weinberg, Dudley: "The Problem of Rabbinic Authority" (1955), pp. 143–150.

ARTICLES IN THE *JOURNAL OF REFORM JUDAISM* (FORMERLY THE *CCAR JOURNAL*)

Ballon, Sydney: "Rabbi's Return" (January 1954), pp. 49–51.

Bamberger, Bernard J.: "The Work of the Modern Rabbi: An Introductory Statement" (April 1953), pp. 7–9.

Bamberger, Henry: "Confessions of an Unashamed Priest" (April 1972), pp. 109–111.

Bernstein, Philip S.: "The Rabbi in Communal and National Activities" (October 1953), pp. 3–6.

Borowitz, Eugene B.: "Restructuring the Rabbinate. An Open Letter to Dr. Theodore I. Lenn" (June 1970), pp. 59–64.

Dreyfus, A. Stanley: "What *Is* the Rabbi to Do?" (October 1962), pp. 46–47.

Eichhorn, David Max: Review of *The Failure of the American Rabbi: A Program for the Revitalization of the Rabbinate in America*, by Sholome Michael Gelber (April 1962), pp. 65–66.

Eisendrath, Maurice N.: "The Authority of the Rabbi" (October 1962), pp. 3–7.

Essrig, Harry: "How Much Longer Shall We Abdicate?" (June 1961), pp. 3–9.

Fein, Leonard J.: "Charisma Is Not Enough" (Autumn 1973), pp. 3–8.

Feinberg, Paul R.: "Some Thoughts on the Rabbi as a Model" (Winter 1979), p. 56.

Feldman, Abraham J.: "*Od Lo Avdah Tikvatenu*: An Invited Comment" (October 1959), pp. 22–26.

———: "Dwelling Together in Harmony" (June 1965), pp. 45–50.

Folkman, Jerome D.: "Can They Trust Their Rabbis?" (April 1964), pp. 21–25.

Friedman, Edwin H.: "Leadership and Self in a Congregational Family" (Winter 1978), pp. 9–25.

Gittelsohn, Roland B.: "Afterthoughts on Lenn: I. The Voice of Every Member" (Winter 1973), pp. 3–8.

————: "On Being a Rabbi: Then and Now" (Spring 1981), pp. 77–88.

Graff, Morris W.: "Rebitzen: An Old Title With a New Meaning" (October 1965), pp. 52–54.

Herscher, Uri D.; Kravitz, Leonard S.; Wohl, Amiel; Kertzer, Morris N.; Levine, Joseph H.; Maller, Allen S.; Landman, Nathan M.; Goldstein, David S.; and Lipman, Eugene J.: "Symposium on the Qualifications of a Rabbi" (January 1972), pp. 2–18.

Herzog, Joseph D.: "Does the Rabbi 'Speak' for the Congregation?" (April 1964), pp. 28–32.

Kaplan, Earl: "The Los Angeles Rabbinic Workshop" (Winter 1979), pp. 57–66.

Katz, Robert L.: "A Rabbi Asks: Concerning a Leader Who Monopolizes" (June 1955), pp. 47–51.

————: "A Rabbi Asks: Shall the Rabbi's Role Be Changed?" (April 1957), pp. 49–53.

————: "A Rabbi Asks: Can a Rabbi Have Personal Friends in His Congregation?" (January 1958), pp. 35–38.

————: "A Rabbi Asks: The Self-Image and the Minority Status of the Rabbi" (April 1959), pp. 46–52.

————: "A Rabbi Asks: On the Role of the Rabbi in City and Suburban Communities" (January 1961), pp. 48–49.

————: "David Caro's Analysis of the Rabbi's Role" (April 1966), pp. 41–46.

————: "The Future of the Rabbinate—Ascribed vs. Achieved Leadership, Perspectives from Sociology" (April 1970), pp. 49–65.

————: "Afterthoughts on Lenn: II. Seminary Malaise" (Winter 1973), pp. 9–18.

————: "Changing Self-Concepts of Reform Rabbis 1976" (Summer 1976), pp. 51–56.

Kline, Alexander S.: "The Rabbi in the Small Town" (April 1954), pp. 10–14.

Kominsky, Neil: "Mixed Marriage: IV. The Role of the Rabbi" (Spring 1973), pp. 4–8.

————: "Rabbinic Ethics and Mixed Marriage: An Exercise in 'Catch-22' " (Autumn 1976), pp. 64–66.

Kravitz, Leonard S.: "Afterthoughts on Lenn: VII. What Does It Mean to Believe in God?" (Winter 1973), pp. 27–31.

Levenson, Paul H.: "The Liberal Chaplain in the Army" (October 1962), pp. 33–37.

Levitsky, Louis M.: "The Rabbi as a Teacher of Judaism" (June 1957), pp. 23–26.

Lipman, Eugene L.: "A Rabbi Asks: Shall the Rabbi's Role Be Changed?" (April 1957), pp. 49–51.

————: "The Myth of the Congregation as Family" (June 1964), pp. 22–26.

————: "Afterthoughts on Lenn: VII. No Surprises" (Winter 1973), pp. 31–33.

Malino, Jerome R.: "The Rabbi's Personal Religion" (April 1954), pp. 15–20.

Markowitz, Samuel H.: "Time and Fulfillment: Some Basic Answers After Thirty-Six Years in the Rabbinate" (April 1959), pp. 19–22.

Marx, Robert J.: "The Problem of Authority in the American Reform Rabbinate—Correspondence" (June 1958), pp. 65–67.

Minda, Albert G.: "The Rabbi in the Pew" (June 1959), pp. 21–24.

Mirsky, Norman: "Unbinding Isaac" (Autumn 1974), pp. 47–52.

Narot, Joseph R.: "The Rabbi and His Human Involvements" (June 1955), pp. 11–14.

————: "Our Urgent Need: Diversity" (Spring 1975), p. 80.

Newman, Louis I.: "Voluntary Gifts for Rabbinical Services" (October 1953), pp. 1–8.

Olan, Levi A.: "A New Evaluation of Rabbinical Seminaries" (June 1967), pp. 4–7.

Oles, M. Arthur: "The Chaplain as Rabbi" (Winter 1977), pp. 76–79.

Passamaneck, Stephen M.: "A Note on Dignity" (June 1971), pp. 76–83.

Petuchowski, Jakob J.: "The Modern Rabbi—A Hundred Years Ago" (January 1963), pp. 33–35.

Plaut, W. Gunther: "New Directions for Reform Rabbis" (October 1971), pp. 24–27.

Raphael, Lawrence W.: "Who Wants to Be a Rabbi and Why?" (Spring 1976), pp. 63–64.

Rapoport, Solomon Judah (translated by Jakob J. Petuchowski): "The Rabbinate—New Style" (June 1959), pp. 27–28.

Regner, Sidney L.: "What's on the Minds of our Men?" (April 1963), pp. 27–30.

————: "The Quest for Authority in Reform Judaism" (Fall 1979), pp. 29–37.

Robins, Andrew J.: "Correspondence" (January 1964), p. 71.

Roseman, Kenneth D.: "American Intellectuals and Clergy" (Winter 1975), pp. 77–84.

————: "Installing the New Rabbi" (Spring 1978), pp. 65–71.

Rubenstein, Byron T.: "A Rabbi Asks: Shall the Rabbi's Role Be Changed?" (April 1957), pp. 51–52.

Rudavsky, Joseph: "Rabbi and Congregation—A Dialogue of Understanding" (June 1963), pp. 26–29.

Rudin, Jacob P.: "The Authority of the Rabbi" (October 1962), pp. 8–10.

Rudin, James A.: "A Modest Proposal" (Winter 1976), pp. 53–55.

Sandler, Robert: "Rabbis Are Not the Only Jews" (Autumn 1976), pp. 77–80.

Sandmel, Samuel: "Rabbis and Recruitment of Rabbinical Students" (April 1960), pp. 45–47.

Schachtel, Hyman Judah: "On the Title 'Rabbi Emeritus' " (Fall 1978), pp. 75–76.

Schindler, Alexander: "Afterthoughts on Lenn: V. A Problem of Communication" (Winter 1973), pp. 21–25.

Schotland, Charles I.: "Social Security for the Rabbi" (January 1955), pp. 6–8.

Schreiber, Mordecai: "Rabbi in Guatemala" (October 1968), pp. 80–89.

Schwartzman, Sylvan D.: "Afterthoughts on Lenn: III. The Religious Vacuum" (Winter 1973), pp. 13–18.

Seltzer, Sanford: "Some Thoughts Concerning the Assistant Rabbi" (January 1964), pp. 38–39.

————: "Some Reflections on Rabbinic-Congregational Relationships" (April 1972), pp. 66–70.

————: "The Complexities of Rabbinical Placement" (Autumn 1976), pp. 58–63.

————: "The Complexities of Rabbinical Placement—Part II" (Winter 1978), pp. 63–67.

Shapero, Sanford M.: "Has the Rabbinate a Future?" (January 1971), pp. 63–66.

Shusterman, Abraham: "The Authority of the Rabbi" (October 1962), pp. 11–13.

Silver, Daniel Jeremy: "Editor's Comments" (October 1966), pp. 2–4.

————: "Editor's Comments" (January 1968), pp. 2–3.

————: "The Worth of the Work We Do" (October 1970), pp. 81–88.

Silver, Harold: "The Changing of the G-d; or, The Relationship of the Rabbi to the Assistant-Associate-Co-Rabbi and Emeritus" (June 1964), pp. 59–66.

Silver, Maxwell: "Retirement as a New Career" (April 1964), pp. 33–39.

Silver, Samuel M.: "Observations of a Quasi-Congregant" (June 1956), pp. 7–9.

Silverman, William B.: "Remember Us Unto Death" (Spring 1974), pp. 41–68.

Singer, Sholom A.: "The $63,000 Question" (June 1971), pp. 31–37.

Siskin, Edgar E.: "The Rabbi in Eclipse" (Spring 1973), pp. 3–13.

Stern, Frank: "North American Reform Rabbis: A Current Sociological Description" (Summer 1980), pp. 32–48.

Stern, Malcolm H.: "Placement—A Depth Report" (January 1972), pp. 23–28.

Tarshish, Allan: "The Authority of the Rabbi" (October 1962), pp. 14–17.

Tedesche, Sidney S.: "Rabbinical Tenure and Contract" (June 1953), pp. 7–9.

Vorspan, David Eli: "Afterthoughts on Lenn: IV. Should Seminarians Share in the Blame?" (Winter 1973), pp. 18–21.

Wax, James A.: Review of *Your Future as a Rabbi*, by Alfred Gottschalk (April 1968), pp. 91–92.

Weinstein, Jacob J.: "Contra Hertzberg: On the Changing American Rabbinate" (June 1966), pp. 70–74.

Wohl, Amiel: "How to Be a Successful Rabbi" (June 1962), pp. 38–40.

Wolf, Arnold Jacob: "The Rabbi and the Failure of the Synagogue" (June 1963), pp. 19–25.

ARTICLES IN *JUDAISM*

Bamberger, Bernard: "The American Rabbi—His Changing Role," III (1954), pp. 488–497.

Borowitz, Eugene B.: "The Future of Rabbinic Training in America," XVIII (1969), pp. 404–405.

Eisenstein, Ira: "The Future of Rabbinic Training in America," XVIII (1969), pp. 401–402.

Goldin, Judah: "The Thinking of the Rabbis," V (1956), pp. 3–12.

Green, Arthur: "The Future of Rabbinic Training in America," XVIII (1969), pp. 405–407.

Hachen, David S.: "The American Reform Rabbi Today," XXIII (Winter 1974), pp. 39–51.

Laderman, Manuel: "A Love Letter to My Congregation," XX (1971), pp. 306–312.

Liebman, Charles S.: "The Future of Rabbinic Training in America," XVIII (1969), pp. 409–410.
Loeb, Mark: "The Future of Rabbinic Training in America," XVIII (1969), pp. 400–401.
Rackman, Emanuel: "The Future of Rabbinic Training in America," XVIII (1969), pp. 402–403.
Siegel, Seymour: "The Future of Rabbinic Training in America," XVIII (1969), pp. 407–408.
Silver, Daniel Jeremy: "The Future of Rabbinic Training in America," XVIII (1969), pp. 390–398.
Weiner, Eugene: "The Future of Rabbinic Training in America," XVIII (1969), pp. 403–404.
Wolf, Arnold Jacob: "The Future of Rabbinic Training in America," XVIII (1969), pp. 387–390.
Zimmerman, Sheldon: "The Future of Rabbinic Training in America," XVIII (1969), pp. 399–400.

ARTICLES IN *RECONSTRUCTIONIST* MAGAZINE

Hollander, B.: "The Rabbinate: In Quest of Professionalism," Vol. 41 (April 1975), pp. 19–25.
Maller, Allen S.: "Rabbi Power," Vol. 36 (December 25, 1970), pp. 19–22.
Prinz, Joachim: "A Rabbi in the Twentieth Century," Vol. 40 (September 1974), pp. 7–15.
Rachlis, A.: "The Aspirations of the Contemporary Rabbi," Vol. 41 (April 1975), pp. 19–25.
Tovin, H.; Skiddell, E.; and Schwarz, S.: "Three Perspectives on the Rabbi's Role," Vol. 46 (July–August 1980), pp. 15–20.

MISCELLANEOUS ARTICLES

Berman, Morton M.: "The Role of the Rabbi: What Was, What Is, and What Shall the Rabbi Be?" (address), (New York: Jewish Institute of Religion, 1941).
Brown, Louis M., and Passamaneck, Stephen S.: "The Rabbis: Preventive Law Lawyers," *Israel Law Review*, Vol. 8, No. 4 (October 1973), pp. 538–549.
Cohon, Samuel S.: "Authority in Judaism," in *Hebrew Union College Annual*, Vol. XI (1936), especially the section "The Rabbis," pp. 614–621; the section "Principles of Rabbinic Authority," pp. 622–627; and the section "Reform Judaism and Authority," pp. 631–646.
Donaldson, J.: "The Title Rabbi in the Gospels—Some Reflections on the Evidence of the Synoptics," *Jewish Quarterly Review*, Vol. 63 (April 1973), pp. 287–291.
England, I.: "Majority Decision vs. Individual Truth," *Tradition*, Vol. 15 (Spring–Summer 1975), pp. 137–152.

Mirsky, Norman: "Rabbinic Dilemmas," in *Jewish Spectator*, Vol. 39 (Spring 1974), pp. 32–36.

Rosenzweig, B.: "The Emergence of the Professional Rabbi in Ashkenazi Jewry," *Tradition*, Vol. 11 (Fall 1970), pp. 22–30.

Saldarini, A. J.: "The End of the Rabbinic Chain of Tradition," *Journal of Biblical Literature*, Vol. 93 (March 1974), pp. 97–106.

Sandmel, Samuel S.: "The Rabbi and His Community," in *Reform Judaism: Essays on Reform Judaism in Britain*, ed. Dow Marmur (London: Alden & Mowbray, 1973).

Shankman, Jacob K.: "The Changing Role of the Rabbi," in *Retrospect and Prospect: Essays in Commemoration of the Seventy-Fifty Anniversary of the Founding of the Central Conference of American Rabbis* (New York: Central Conference of American Rabbis, 1965), pp. 230–251.

"Why I Chose to Be a Rabbi," *Menorah Journal*, Vol. II (1916), pp. 301–307.